Warmth & Wisdom
LEGACY OF SCRAP QUILTS

AT *Leisure Arts*, WE BELIEVE THAT THE HISTORY OF QUILTS AND QUILTING *HAS ONLY JUST BEGUN.*

After all, the very reasons our grandmothers chose to quilt are why we still sew scraps of fabric into warm and memorable blankets today. So as long as there is a love of family and community, a desire for beauty, and a need for creativity, there are sure to be quilters.

In this book, we explore the intriguing characteristics of fourteen scrap quilts from the past. We also offer seven modern interpretations of some of these patchwork treasures, and we would like to share with you the thought-provoking quotes and tender recollections we've discovered along the way. It is our sincere hope that the patterns in this publication will enrich your creative experiences so that your loved ones will also enjoy the LEGACY OF SCRAP QUILTS.

Wishing you a *Lifetime* of HAPPY STITCHING,

Sandra Case

SANDRA CASE
Vice President and Editor-in-Chief
Leisure Arts, Inc.
Little Rock, Arkansas

Thank You

We would like to extend our thanks to the staff of the Historic Arkansas Museum for the use of the photographs on pages 8 and 9. And we are grateful to the New Hampshire Historical Society for the 1859 county survey map image of the Cocheco Mills in Dover, New Hampshire.

A special "thank you" goes to Janet Brandt for loaning us her feedsack quilt and her mother's photo of the Ladies Aide group of Grace Mennonite Church in Chicago, Illinois. Our thanks also go to Patricia Uhiren for the loan of her yellow basket quilt and for sharing her memories of Walter Sommer. Feedsack fabrics shown throughout this book are the property of Sondra Curtis, Guinn Trogden, and Beulah Wright — thank you, ladies!

We greatly appreciate Julie Schrader for the expert machine quilting on the contemporary quilts. We also thank the quilters who pieced the new quilt tops: Larcie Burnett, Patty Galas, Nelwyn Gray, Marie Hanley, Judith Hassed, Judie Kline, Valerie Schramel, and Glenda Taylor.

Editorial Staff

Vice President and Editor-in-Chief: Sandra Graham Case. *Executive Director of Publications:* Cheryl Nodine Gunnells. *Senior Publications Director:* Susan White Sullivan. *Publications Operations Director:* Cheryl Johnson. *Editorial Director:* Susan Frantz Wiles. *Photography Director:* Karen Hall. *Art Operations Director:* Jeff Curtis. TECHNICAL — *Technical Editor:* Lisa Lancaster. *Technical Writer:* Jean Lewis. EDITORIAL — *Associate Editor:* Susan McManus Johnson. ART — *Art Publications Director:* Rhonda Shelby. *Art Imaging Director:* Mark Hawkins. *Art Category Manager:* Lora Puls. *Lead Graphic Artist:* Jenny Dickerson. *Graphic Artists:* Dayle Carozza, Amy Gerke, Stephanie Hamling, and Brittany Skarda. DESIGN — *Lead Designer:* Linda Tiano. *Photostylists:* Sondra Daniel, Janna Laughlin, and Cassie Newsome. *Staff Photographer:* Russell Ganser. *Publishing Systems Administrator:* Becky Riddle. *Publishing Systems Assistants:* Clint Hanson, Myra S. Means, and Chris Wertenberger.

Business Staff

Publisher: Rick Barton. *Vice President, Finance:* Tom Siebenmorgen. *Director of Corporate Planning and Development:* Laticia Dittrich. *Vice President, Retail Marketing:* Bob Humphrey. *Vice President, Sales:* Ray Shelgosh. *Vice President, National Accounts:* Pam Stebbins. *Director of Sales and Services:* Margaret Reinold. *Vice President, Operations:* Jim Dittrich. *Comptroller, Operations:* Rob Thieme. *Retail Customer Service Manager:* Stan Raynor. *Print Production Manager:* Fred F. Pruss.

Made in the United States of America

ISBN 1-57486-351-7
10 9 8 7 6 5 4 3 2 1

Contents

IN ONE FORM OR ANOTHER, *Quilts* HAVE BEEN AROUND FOR ALMOST AS LONG AS MANKIND HAS KNOWN HOW TO TURN *fibers* INTO *cloth*.

The earliest quilted garment was discovered in a tomb in Egypt. And quilted underclothes were a necessity for Medieval knights — while their armor protected them from enemy assault, their skin needed protection from the chaffing and pinching their metal suits could inflict! In either of these instances, quilting was a costly activity and only the wealthy could afford to own quilted clothing. This was still true centuries later in Colonial America when woven blankets and rugs were the cheapest way to cover a bed. To own a real quilt, either wholecloth or patchwork, took "deep pockets" that the average American didn't have. It was also quicker to simply weave blankets just as they wove home-spun fabric for clothing.

Young America
LEARNS TO QUILT

Cocheco Falls Mills, Dover, NH

Courtesy of NEW HAMPSHIRE HISTORICAL SOCIETY

IN THE MID-1800'S, THE ESTABLISHMENT OF NEW ENGLAND'S TEXTILE MILLS made printed cotton fabric easier to acquire in America. Even so, clothing was still the primary goal of seamstresses, and quilts were usually made from fabric scraps or worn-out garments.

A number of the dyes used in fabrics before the 1870's were "fugitive" or non-colorfast, leaving the modern quilter to wonder why those early quilts were so drab. The truth is, an 1850's quilter enjoyed working with bright fabrics just as we do today, and she sometimes dyed her fabrics to get the shades she wanted. The color sources she used were as common as walnut shells, onion skins, or clay. A popular color fixative was lead, that element so detrimental to human health! Also hindering the nineteenth century quilter was the need to create her own quilt padding. Unspun cotton or wool was usually carded into "batts" for this purpose, but old blankets were often used, and even leaves and corn husks! And yet, with all the extra effort required of the quilter, the 1850's saw the first widespread quilting craze.

Westward Migration & The Album Quilt

WHILE FRONTIER MEN SET THEIR SIGHTS ON HOMESTEADING THE WEST, **FRONTIER WOMEN** PRESERVED MEMORIES of loved ones back East by stitching or writing their names on the blocks of album quilts. These blocks often contained scraps of clothing from friends and family, and were sometimes completed as gifts to the travelers before they departed. When these young women made their new homes in the untamed mountains and prairies, it must have been a great comfort to rest under those blankets of love. ❋

- Quilting Bees -

AS **AMERICA STRETCHED ITS BORDERS** AND NEW LAND WAS CLAIMED, SEWING WAS OFTEN REDUCED TO A **SURVIVAL SKILL.** The desire and opportunity to do creative stitching were necessarily merged with the production of practical items for the household. Patchwork quilts were ideal outlets for creative energies. And yet, the last stitches of a quilt top were likely to be finished quickly in anticipation of its "putting in" — the common phrase for when a pieced top was placed in a quilt frame along with batting and backing. Once a quilt reached this stage, it was time for an important social event.

FOR PIONEER WOMEN, QUILTING BEES WERE LONGED-FOR OPPORTUNITIES TO VISIT WITH NEIGHBORS, SHARE GOOD FOOD, AND CATCH UP ON NEWS FROM BACK EAST. And for women everywhere, a quilting bee was sometimes a CHANCE TO SPEAK FREELY without the presence of their menfolk. It was at a quilting bee on the east coast that SUSAN B. ANTHONY first spoke about equality for women. One wonders if Ms. Anthony would be surprised to learn how many women still enjoy quilting almost a century after "GETTING THE VOTE." And how many of today's quilters might find themselves agreeing with Grandma's sentiments as they read EUGENE FIELD'S POEM "GRANDMA'S PRAYER"?

Grandma's Prayer
EUGENE FIELD (1850-1895)

I pray that, risen from the dead,
I may in glory stand—
A crown, perhaps, upon my head,
But a needle in my hand.

I've never learned to sing or play,
So let no harp be mine;
From birth unto my dying day,
Plain sewing's been my line.

Therefore, accustomed to the end
To plying useful stitches,
I'll be content if asked to mend
The little angel's breeches.

FROM
Victoriana ...

QUEEN VICTORIA OF ENGLAND HAD FAR-REACHING INFLUENCE ON THE FASHIONS OF HER DAY. When she married in 1840, every young bride wanted to wear a dress like hers. Crazy quilts, with their rich fabrics of silk, satin, and velvet, reflected the opulence of Victoria's wardrobe. And when the Queen's beloved husband died in 1861, entire nations found themselves wearing shades of grey and black. Mourning prints rose in popularity, and quilts from the late 1800's are often punctuated with scraps of the somber fabrics.

IDA FERGUSON LEWIS of *Hot Springs, Arkansas*, posed in front of her ROMAN CROSS VARIATION QUILT around the year 1900. Wearing a solemn expression for the camera was the custom of the day, which reminds us of this quote from another quilter, possibly of Ida's era:

"What with rearin' a family, and tendin' to a home, and all my chores — that quilt was a long time in the frame. The story of my life is pieced into it. All my joys and all my sorrows."

From the collection of **HISTORIC ARKANSAS MUSEUM**, *Little Rock, Arkansas*
Accession Number 95.064.0002

LESSIE CAMERON BRAKEFIELD of *Doddridge, Arkansas*, had reason to be proud of her accomplishments on the day this photo was taken. Her very young hands made the wholecloth quilt behind her. The photo was taken around 1910. We wonder if Lessie was familiar with the words of this traditional verse:

At your quilting, maids, don't tarry.
Quilt quick if you would marry.
A maid who is quiltless at twenty-one,
Never shall greet her bridal sun.

From the collection of **HISTORIC ARKANSAS MUSEUM**, *Little Rock, Arkansas*
Accession Number 95.064.0001

... TO *Nostalgia*

BY CONTRAST, THE FIRST DECADE OF THE **TWENTIETH CENTURY** SAW AMERICAN QUILTERS TURNING BACK TO THEIR NATION'S EARLIEST DAYS FOR DESIGN INSPIRATION. The quilters of 1918 rejoiced over the end of World War I, and they became fascinated by the idea of Colonial quilts — despite the fact that quilts were a rarity in the earliest days of America. Using the oldest patterns they could find, post-war quilters created floral and botanical quilts and a revival of the charm quilt that was popular in their grandmothers' time. Through the 1920's and 30's, conversation prints underwent a great deal of change, replacing the nineteenth-century motifs of horseshoes and flags with playful children and nursery images.

"Make Do OR DO WITHOUT."

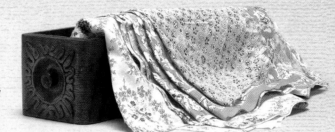

*I*N 1930, THE **GREAT DEPRESSION** HAD JUST BEGUN. SINCE THERE WAS NO EXCESS FABRIC TO BE FOUND IN MOST HOUSEHOLDS, **TRUE SCRAP QUILTS WERE POPULAR ONCE AGAIN.** AND YET, QUILTERS REJOICED IN THE COLORFAST FABRICS

that did come their way — even when the source was ORDINARY FEEDSACKS. Traditional white feedsacks were introduced after the invention of the sewing machine in 1846. But in the early 1900's, manufacturers realized that women were more likely to purchase animal feed in colorful printed bags. After all, a full-size feedsack contained a little over a yard of fabric, and the average dress of the 1930's needed only four sacks to complete it. Flour and sugar producers also made bags from softer, more closely woven fabric. The trend was set, and the cheery feedsack motifs of the 1920's and 1930's were made into curtains, tablecloths, towels — even underwear! And of course, the leftover scraps from all this sewing became the wonderful patchwork quilts that, for at least one generation, created memories of sleeping under fabric mosaics in shades of bubblegum pink and apple green. ⋘

THE **DESIRE TO** *Help Others*

IS AN ADMIRABLE CHARACTERISTIC FOUND IN

EVERY *Generation* OF **QUILTERS**.

IONA LEVREAU (far right) SHARES THIS CIRCA 1950 PHOTO OF HER **LADIES AIDE GROUP**. The women were members of the GRACE MENNONITE CHURCH of Chicago, Illinois, and the FRIENDSHIP QUILT they proudly display is a product of their teamwork. Each of the women embroidered a block of the quilt and brought it to one of the monthly quilting bees. The individual blocks were then sewn together and quilted. The finished blanket was sent to missionaries overseas, along with the good wishes of the industrious Ladies Aide.

Everything Old
IS NEW AGAIN

QUILTING FADED FROM POPULARITY IN THE YEARS FOLLOWING THE **SECOND WORLD WAR**. HOWEVER, A SKILL SO CLOSELY ASSOCIATED WITH OUR NATION'S HISTORY IS NOT EASILY FORGOTTEN. In 1976, patriotism in the wake of the United States Bicentennial celebrations brought a surge of interest in the handicrafts of yesteryear. Quilts were once again produced, this time by the blue-jean wearing descendents of the pioneers. Yet, rather than wane as the years passed, the new quilting trend has grown larger and more diverse.

TODAY'S QUILTER HAS THE LUXURY OF CHOOSING FROM THOUSANDS OF TRADITIONAL AND **CONTEMPORARY QUILT PATTERNS** AND FABRICS. With modern sewing conveniences and never-ending textile innovations, it seems there is no limit to the amount of detail, depth of color, and range of texture that can be achieved in quilts.

AND YET THERE REMAIN A FEW **DRY GOODS PRODUCERS** WHO STILL USE **COLORFUL COTTON SACKS** TO PACKAGE GRAINS, FLOUR, AND SUGAR. Why is this? You have only to browse the Internet to see that the demand for vintage fabrics is at an all-time high. Check out the online auctions and you will see that homespun fabrics — those that were actually created on a hand loom in the 1800's — are also fetching high prices, even though it is difficult to verify their age or authenticity. Modern quilters are eager to rediscover elements of their stitching history, and it would seem as though feedsacks of any era can only become more valuable with time.

SO WHAT DOES OUR **SCRAP QUILT LEGACY** MEAN? Scrap quilts remind us that difficult times can and should be met with creativity and perseverance. In our own age, we see that quilts are not only beautiful works of art created in an endless array of colors and patterns — quilts are also about compassion, hope, and possibilities. Perhaps these qualities have always been the TRUE WARMTH of all quilts. And perhaps this is the WISDOM that all quilters, across all ages, will always share.

Double Wedding Ring

THE ELEGANT DOUBLE WEDDING RING PATTERN WAS VERY

POPULAR IN THE 1920's AND 1930's. The machine-sewn binding of this quilt

looks like purchased bias tape and some of the fabric pieces may be from the

1950's. And there may be scraps of old feedsacks scattered among the calico.

Because of the many curved seams and small pieces, this pattern could only have

been executed by an experienced seamstress. However, the large stitches used

to quilt the intricate design show the same impatience to be finished as seen on

the Maple Leaf Quilt (page 50). Over all, this is still a beautiful piece of sewing

with many hours of work and probably a great deal of love

going into each seam. With modern sewing techniques,

you can piece your Double Wedding Ring much more

quickly, leaving you more time for quilting it.

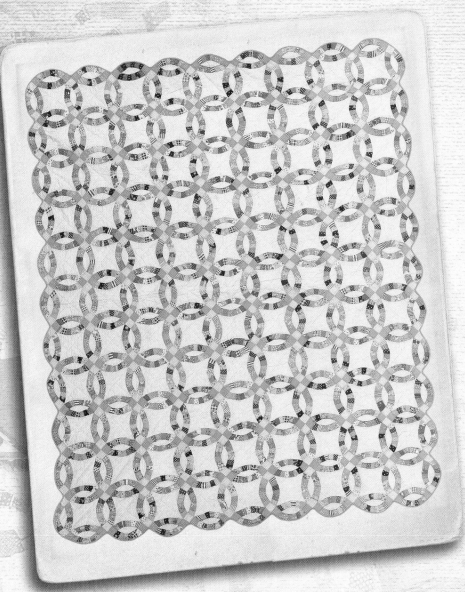

Double Wedding Ring Quilt

SKILL LEVEL: 1 2 3 4 5

QUILT SIZE: 67 3/8" x 81 3/8" (171 cm x 207 cm)

FINISHED BLOCK SIZE: 10" diameter (25 cm)

PIECED BLOCKS: 99

·CLASSIC·

Yardage Requirements

Yardage is based on 45"w fabric.
$^1/_2$ yd (46 cm) of pink solid
$^1/_2$ yd (46 cm) of green solid
9 yds (8.2 m) **total** of assorted prints
$6^1/_2$ yds (5.9 m) of cream solid
5 yds (4.6 m) of backing fabric
$^7/_8$ yd (80 cm) of binding fabric
76" x 90" (193 cm x 229 cm) rectangle
 of batting

Cutting Out the Pieces

Refer to **Rotary Cutting***, page 133, to cut strips. All measurements include a* $^1/_4$*" seam allowance. Refer to* **Template Cutting***, page 135, to use patterns, page 21.*
From pink solid:
- Cut 9 **strips** $1^5/_8$"w. From these **strips**, cut 216 **squares** $1^5/_8$" x $1^5/_8$".

From green solid:
- Cut 9 **strips** $1^5/_8$"w. From these **strips**, cut 220 **squares** $1^5/_8$" x $1^5/_8$".

From assorted prints:
- Cut 1744 of **template A**.
- Cut 436 of **template B**.
- Cut 436 of **template B reversed**.

From cream solid:
- Cut 218 of **template C**.
- Cut 99 of **template D**.

Assembling the Quilt Top

1. Sew 1 **B**, 4 **A's** and 1 **B reversed** together to make **Unit 1**. Make 436 **Unit 1's**.

Unit 1
(make 436)

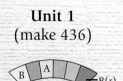

2. Sew 1 pink **square** to each end of a **Unit 1** to make **Unit 2**. Make 108 **Unit 2's**.

Unit 2
(make 108)

3. Sew 1 green **square** to each end of a **Unit 1** to make **Unit 3**. Make 110 **Unit 3's**.

Unit 3
(make 110)

Note: For curved seams in **Steps 3 - 8***, match centers and pin at center and at dots, then match and pin between these points. Sew seams with cream background pieces (***C** *or* **D***) on top, easing in fullness from pieced units.*

4. Sew 1 **Unit 1** and 1 **C** together to make **Unit 4**. Make 218 **Unit 4's**.

Unit 4
(make 218)

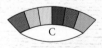

5. Sew 1 **Unit 2** and 1 **Unit 4** together to make **Unit 5**. Make 108 **Unit 5's**.

Unit 5
(make 108)

6. Sew 1 **Unit 3** and 1 **Unit 4** together to make **Unit 6**. Make 110 **Unit 6's**.

Unit 6
(make 110)

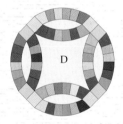

7. Referring to **Wedding Ring Block Diagram**, sew 2 **Unit 5's**, 2 **Unit 6's** and 1 D together to make **Wedding Ring Block**. Make 50 **Blocks**.

Wedding Ring Block
(make 50)

8. Referring to **Setting Block Diagrams**, sew 1 **Unit 5** and 1 **D** together to make **Top/Bottom Setting Block**. Make 8 **Top/Bottom Setting Blocks**. Sew 1 **Unit 6** and 1 **D** together to make **Side Setting Block**. Make 10 **Side Setting Blocks**.

Top/Bottom Setting Block
(make 8)

Side Setting Block
(make 10)

9. Referring to **Assembly Diagram**, page 19, sew **Wedding Ring Blocks**, **Setting Blocks** and remaining **D's** together into horizontal **Rows**. Sew **Rows** together to complete **Quilt Top**.

Completing the Quilt

1. Follow **Quilting**, page 138, to mark, layer and quilt as desired. Our quilt is hand quilted in the ditch around the rings. There is an "X" quilted in the center of each ring.
2. To prepare quilt for binding, straight stitch around quilt ⅛" from raw edge. Trim backing and batting even with raw edge of quilt top.
3. Cut a 29" square of binding fabric. Follow **Making Continuous Bias Binding**, page 141, to make approximately 10 yards of 2"w bias binding.
4. Follow **Steps 1** and **2** of **Attaching Binding with Mitered Corners**, page 142, to pin binding to front of quilt, easing binding around curved edges. Sew binding to quilt until binding overlaps beginning end by approximately 2". Trim excess binding. Fold binding over to quilt backing and pin in place, covering stitching line. Blindstitch binding to backing.

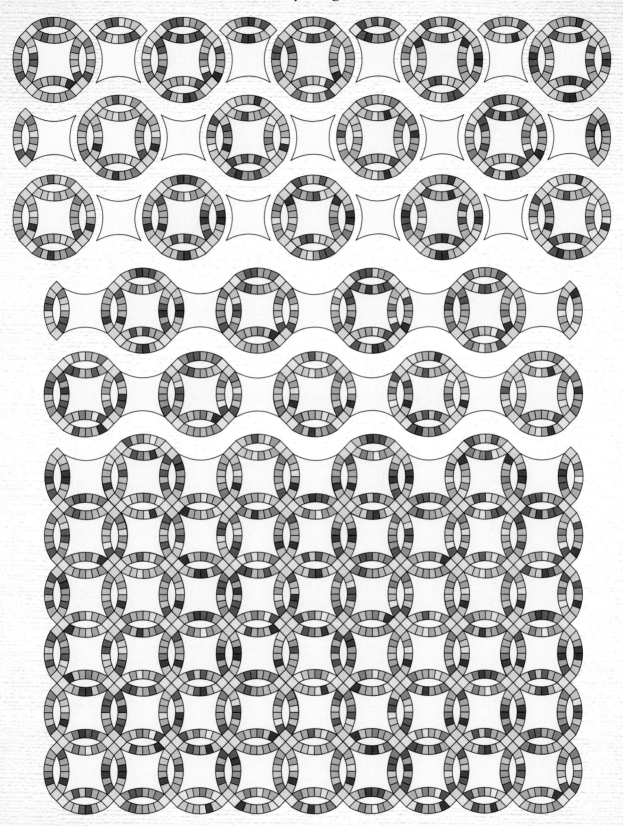

Quilt Top Diagram

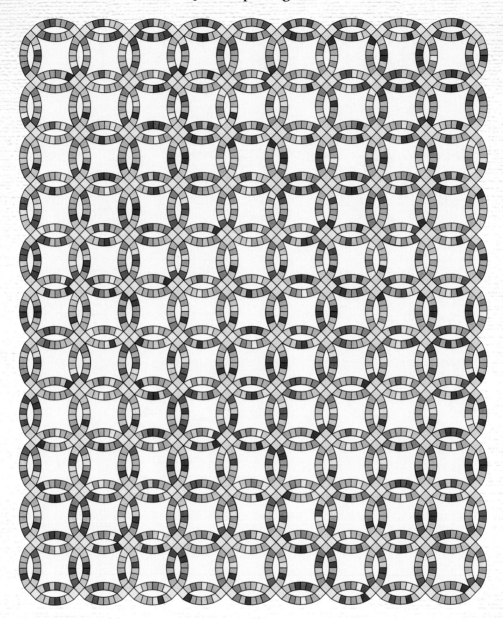

SHUT OUT ALL OF **YOUR PAST** EXCEPT THAT WHICH

 WILL HELP YOU *weather* YOUR TOMORROWS.

∽ Helen Keller

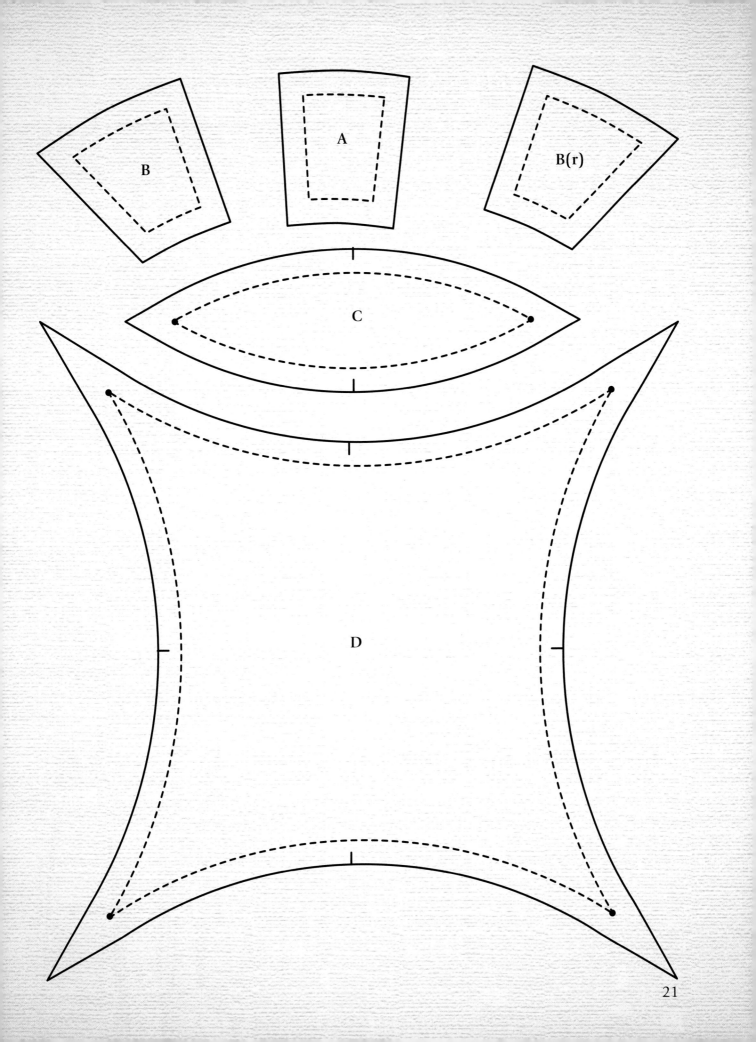

Schoolhouse

THIS QUILT BLOCK IS **KNOWN BY SEVERAL NAMES.** **"TIPPECANOE"** and **"LINCOLN'S CABIN HOME"** are titles with historical significance. And "OLD KENTUCKY HOME" was inspired by a song written in the 1850's that eventually became the state song of Kentucky. An interesting feature of this circa 1890-1920 quilt is its unusual backing. It is composed of several picture panels sewn together, each featuring a Dutch woman with her children. A few of these soft, closely woven fabric panels have the word "Hamilton" in white relief. The original purpose of this fabric is unknown, but we speculate that it may be handkerchief fabric meant to be cut apart and hemmed. The entire quilt is tied rather than quilted, and the binding is machine sewn.

Schoolhouse Quilt

SKILL LEVEL: 1 2 3 4 5

QUILT SIZE: 67" x 72½" (170 cm x 184 cm)

FINISHED BLOCK SIZE: 9" x 9" (23 cm x 23 cm)

PIECED BLOCKS: 30

· CLASSIC ·

Yardage Requirements

Yardage is based on 45"w fabric.

10" x 14" (25 cm x 36 cm) scrap of 30 light prints or solids

12" x 16" (30 cm x 41 cm) scrap of 30 dark prints or solids

$2^1/_2$ yds (2.3 m) of burgundy print

$4^1/_2$ yds (4.1 m) of backing fabric

$^7/_8$ yd (80 cm) of binding fabric

75" x 81" (191 cm x 206 cm) rectangle of batting

You will also need:

Black pearl cotton

Cutting Out the Pieces

*To make this quilt easier to piece, our patterns eliminate the need for set-in seams. Follow **Rotary Cutting**, page 133, to cut fabric. Follow **Template Cutting**, page 135, to use patterns, page 28. Cut long sashing strips along the lengthwise grain of the fabric before cutting short sashing strips. All measurements include a $^1/_4$" seam allowance.*

From *each* light print or solid:
- Cut 2 rectangles $2^3/_8$" x 2" (**A**).
- Cut 1 rectangle $3^3/_4$" x 2" (**B**).
- Cut 1 of **template C**. Cut 1 of **template C** reversed.
- Cut 1 of **template D**.
- Cut 1 rectangle 5" x 1" (**E**).
- Cut 3 rectangles $1^1/_4$" x $3^3/_4$" (**F**).
- Cut 1 rectangle $1^1/_4$" x $5^3/_4$" (**G**).

From *each* dark print or solid:
- Cut 1 of **template H**.
- Cut 1 of **template I**.
- Cut 2 rectangles $1^1/_2$" x 2" (**J**).
- Cut 1 rectangle $4^1/_4$" x $1^3/_4$" (**K**).
- Cut 3 rectangles 2" x $3^3/_4$" (**L**).
- Cut 2 rectangles $1^1/_4$" x $3^3/_4$" (**M**).
- Cut 2 rectangles 5" x $1^1/_4$" (**N**).
- Cut 1 rectangle $4^1/_4$" x $1^1/_4$" (**O**).

From burgundy print:
- Cut 6 **long sashing strips** 4" x 72".
- Cut 25 **short sashing strips** 4" x $9^1/_2$".

Assembling the Quilt Top

*Follow **Piecing and Pressing**, page 135, to assemble the quilt top.*

1. Sew 2 **A's**, 2 **J's**, and 1 **B** together to make **Unit 1**.

Unit 1
(make 1)

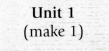

2. Sew 1 **C**, 1 **H**, 1 **D**, 1 **I**, and 1 **C reversed** together to make **Unit 2**.

Unit 2
(make 1)

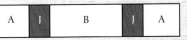

3. Sew 2 **L's** and 1 **F** together. Add 1 **K** and 1 **O** to make **Unit 3**.

Unit 3
(make 1)

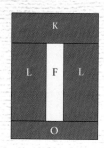

4. Sew 2 **M's**, 2 **F's**, and 1 **L** together. Add 2 **N's** and 1 **E** to make **Unit 4**.

Unit 4
(make 1)

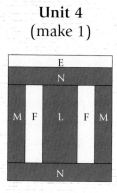

5. Sew **Unit 3**, 1 **G**, and **Unit 4** together to make **Unit 5**.

Unit 5
(make 1)

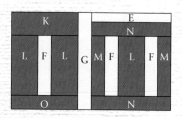

6. Referring to **Block Diagram**, sew **Units 1, 2, and 5** together to complete **Schoolhouse Block**.

Schoolhouse Block

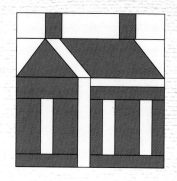

7. Repeat **Steps 1-6** to make a total of 30 **Schoolhouse Blocks**.

8. Refer to **Assembly Diagram**, page 27, to sew 6 **Schoolhouse Blocks** and 5 **Short Sashing Strips** into **Vertical Rows**. Make 5 **Vertical Rows**.

9. Keeping horizontal sashing strips aligned, sew **Rows** and **Long Sashing Strips** together to complete piecing the **Quilt Top**.

Completing the Quilt

1. Follow **Quilting**, page 138, to mark, layer and quilt as desired. Our quilt is tied with pearl cotton in the seams between the blocks and sashings and in the center of each Schoolhouse.

2. Cut a 28" square of binding fabric. Follow **Binding**, page 141, to bind quilt using 2^1/$_2$"w bias binding with mitered corners.

THE **INVARIABLE MARK** OF *wisdom*

IS TO SEE THE *miraculous* IN THE **COMMON**.

Ralph Waldo Emerson, 1836

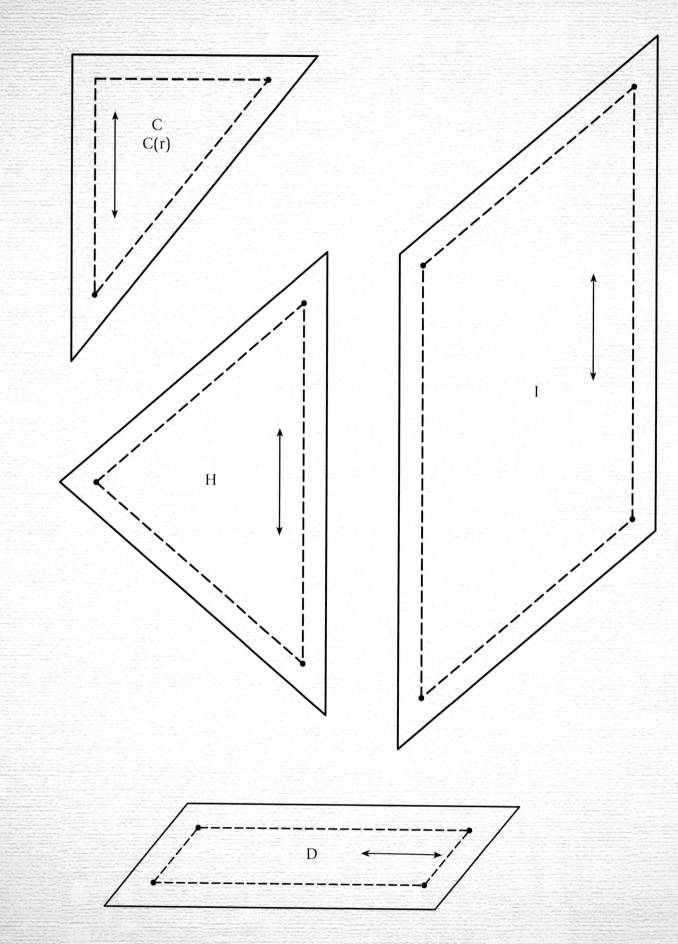

C
C(r)

H

I

D

A *Curmudgeon's* SECRET

PATTI UHIREN, *A NATIVE OF WISCONSIN*, SHARES THIS STORY ABOUT THE **SPECIAL PLACE** A QUILT HAS IN **HER FAMILY'S HISTORY**.

Patti's GREAT-UNCLE WALTER worked on the family dairy farm, never leaving it except to serve in the first World War. He married a young woman named MYRTLE early in the 1930's, but lost her to illness before they ever had children. After Myrtle's death, Walter became a recluse, a gruff and embittered man. On rare occasions, Patti would go with her father to spend time with Walter. The visits softened the old man's outlook just a little, and in later years Patti brought her own daughter to visit her aging great-uncle. When Walter passed away in 1985, he left the farm and his few belongings to Patti's father.

Among these was a trunk that Walter kept in his spartan, unheated bedroom. When the family opened the trunk, they discovered it was actually Myrtle's hope chest which had not been opened in many years. Patti and her family were astonished to see the great care that Walter, a seemingly cold and gruff man, had taken of his wife's fondest possessions. Among these was a yellow basket quilt, a Christmas gift from Myrtle's parents that still has its gift tag all these decades later. Patti counts the quilt as one of her most prized possessions, for who couldn't love a quilt that was once hidden in the softness of an old curmudgeon's heart?

Appliquéd Butterflies

WAS THIS PRETTY COLLECTION OF BUTTERFLIES

created for a little girl? The purple inner borders and colorful insects seem like just the thing to please a young miss. The black embroidery floss Blanket Stitches used on this quilt were a popular way of appliquéing pieces in the years between 1910 and 1925. Running Stitches were used to form the antennae and French Knots for the eyes. The quilting is done in a feather design, and the scalloped edge of the outer border may have been produced by using a dinner plate for the pattern.

Appliquéd Butterflies

SKILL LEVEL: 1 2 3 4 5

QUILT SIZE: 76¹/₂" x 87" (194 cm x 221 cm)

FINISHED BLOCK SIZE: 10¹/₂" x 10¹/₂" (27 cm x 27 cm)

APPLIQUÉD BLOCKS: 24

· CLASSIC ·

Yardage Requirements

Yardage is based on 45"w fabric.
- 5$\frac{1}{8}$ yds (4.7 m) of white solid
- 4 yds (3.7 m) of lavender solid
- 9" x 9" (23 cm x 23 cm) scrap of 24 assorted prints or solids
- 5$\frac{3}{8}$ yds (4.9 m) of backing fabric
- $\frac{7}{8}$ yd (80 cm) of binding fabric
- 85" x 95" (216 cm x 241 cm) rectangle of batting

You will also need:
- Paper-backed fusible web
- Black embroidery floss

Cutting Out the Pieces

*Follow **Preparing Fusible Appliqués**, page 137, to use butterfly pattern, page 35. Refer to **Rotary Cutting**, page 133, to cut fabric. Cut borders first along the lengthwise grain of the fabric. All measurements include a $\frac{1}{4}$" seam allowance.*

From white solid:
- Cut 2 **side outer borders** 7" x 93$\frac{1}{2}$".
- Cut 2 **top and bottom outer borders** 7" x 83".
- Cut 24 **squares** 12" x 12".

From lavender solid:
- Cut 2 **side middle borders** 5$\frac{3}{4}$" x 93$\frac{1}{2}$".
- Cut 2 **top and bottom middle borders** 5$\frac{3}{4}$" x 83".
- Cut 2 **side inner borders** 5$\frac{3}{4}$" x 49".
- Cut 2 **top and bottom inner borders** 5$\frac{3}{4}$" x 38$\frac{1}{2}$".

From each scrap of print or solid:
- Cut 1 **butterfly**.

Assembling the Quilt Top

*Follow **Piecing and Pressing**, page 135, to assemble the quilt top.*

1. Center, then fuse 1 **butterfly** onto each white square. Referring to **Embroidery Stitches**, page 144, and **Block Diagram**, Blanket Stitch around **butterflies** using 2 strands of black floss. Use a Running Stitch to add detail lines and antenna to **butterflies**. Make 2 French Knot eyes.

Block Diagram

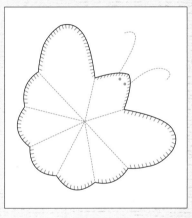

2. Trim **Blocks** to 11" x 11". Referring to **Quilt Top Diagram**, page 34, sew 6 **Blocks** together to make quilt center.
3. Follow **Adding Mitered Borders**, page 138, to sew **inner borders** to quilt center.

4. Sew 4 **Blocks** together in a vertical row to make **Unit 1**. Make 2 **Unit 1's.**

Unit 1
(make 2)

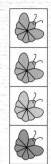

5. Sew 5 **Blocks** together in a horizontal row to make **Unit 2**. Make 2 **Unit 2's.**

Unit 2
(make 2)

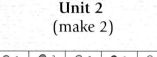

6. Referring to **Quilt Top Diagram**, sew 1 **Unit 1** to each side of quilt center. Sew 1 **Unit 2** to the top, then bottom edges of quilt center.
7. Sew **middle** and **outer borders** together to make 4 **border sets.** Follow **Adding Mitered Borders**, page 138, to sew **border sets** to quilt center.

Scallop Border Diagram

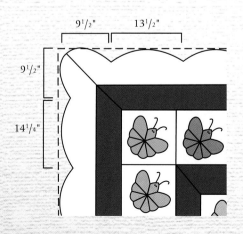

1. Referring to **Marking Quilting Lines**, page 139, and **Scallop Border Diagram**, mark cutting line for scallops on **Quilt Top**. Refer to **Quilting**, page 138, to mark, layer, and quilt as desired. Our quilt is hand quilted with cross hatching in the blocks and a feathered scallop in the borders.
2. To prepare quilt for binding, straight stitch around quilt $^1/_8$" inside the scallop cutting line. Trim backing, batting, and quilt top on marked cutting line.
3. Cut a $30^1/_2$" square of binding fabric. Follow **Making Continuous Bias Strip Binding**, page 141, to make 2"w bias binding.
4. Follow **Steps 1** and **2** of **Attaching Binding with Mitered Corners**, page 142, to pin binding to front of quilt, easing binding around curved edges. Sew binding to quilt until binding overlaps beginning end by approximately 2". Trim excess binding. Fold binding over to quilt backing and pin in place, covering stitching line. Blindstitch binding to backing.

Quilt Top Diagram

Butterfly

Grandmother's Flower Garden

THIS VERY POPULAR 1930'S QUILT DESIGN HAS ALSO BEEN CALLED BRIDE'S BOUQUET, GARDEN WALK, MARTHA WASHINGTON'S FLOWER GARDEN, AND THE WHEEL OF LIFE.

Since each block is composed of 37 hexagonal pieces, minimal use of printed fabric is an important feature of the overall design — but don't let the number of pieces worry you about the time involved. Our instructions are for ENGLISH PAPER PIECING, an ingenious method that guarantees even seams and fast construction. If you enjoy hand piecing, these blocks are ideal for take-along projects.

Grandmother's Flower Garden

SKILL LEVEL: 1 2 **3** 4 5

QUILT SIZE: 76¼" x 98½" (194 cm x 250 cm)

FINISHED BLOCK SIZE: 12¼" x 10" (31 cm x 25 cm)

PIECED BLOCKS: 53

· CLASSIC ·

Yardage Requirements

Yardage is based on 45"w fabric.

- $^3/_8$ yd (34 cm) of yellow solid
- $^1/_8$ yd (11 cm) **each** of 53 different prints
- 6" x 8"(15 cm x 20 cm) scrap of coordinating solid for **each** print
- $4^3/_8$ yds (4 m) of green solid
- $3^1/_4$ yds (2.9 m) of white solid
- 6 yds (5.5 m) of backing fabric
- $^7/_8$ yd (80 cm) of binding fabric

You will also need:

- 85" x 107" (216 cm x 272 cm) rectangle of batting
- 1" (2.54 cm) pre-cut paper hexagons*

Cutting Out the Pieces

*Refer to **Rotary Cutting**, page 133, to cut fabric. All measurements include a $^1/_4$" seam allowance.*

From yellow solid:
- Cut 4 **strips** $2^1/_4$"w. From these **strips**, cut 53 **rectangles** $2^1/_4$" x $2^5/_8$".

From *each* print fabric:
- Cut 1 **strip** $2^1/_4$"w. From this **strip**, cut 12 **rectangles** $2^1/_4$" x $2^5/_8$".

From *each* scrap of solid fabric:
- Cut 2 **strips** $2^1/_4$"w. From these **strips**, cut 6 **rectangles** $2^1/_4$" x $2^5/_8$".

From green solid:
- Cut 62 **strips** $2^1/_4$"w. From these **strips**, cut 978 **rectangles** $2^1/_4$" x $2^5/_8$".

From white solid:
- Cut 48 **strips** $2^1/_4$"w. From these **strips**, cut 766 **rectangles** $2^1/_4$" x $2^5/_8$".

*After cutting the number of rectangles needed from each fabric, stack 4 rectangles. Center and pin a paper hexagon to top rectangle. Using a rotary cutter and small acrylic ruler and leaving a $^1/_4$" seam allowance on each side, trim corners from rectangles as shown in **Cutting Diagram**. Repeat to cut number of hexagons needed from each fabric.*

Cutting Diagram

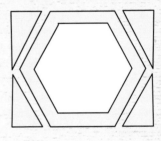

Traditionally, one paper and one fabric hexagon are cut for each of the 2,751 hexagons used in the quilt. To speed the cutting process, we used pre-cut paper hexagons and rotary cut the fabric hexagons. The paper hexagons can be re-used up to 3 times, reducing the total needed to 917. **Hint: Lightly spray starch and dry iron used hexagons before re-use.*

*If you choose to make freezer paper templates, refer to **Template Cutting**, page 135, to use hexagon pattern, page 41. Cut freezer paper into 138 sheets $8^1/_2$" x 11".*

*Trace around template 20 times on dull side of 23 sheets. With 1 traced sheet on top and shiny sides down, stack 6 sheets of freezer paper together. To hold the sheets together, touch the tip of a hot iron to the center of each hexagon; cut out paper hexagons. Repeat with remaining sheets. Follow **Cutting Out the Pieces** to cut fabric. Center hexagons, shiny side down, on the wrong side of each fabric rectangle and iron to rectangle; trim fabric corners as described in **Cutting Diagram**. Follow remainder of instructions to complete Quilt.*

Making the Flower Blocks

For each Flower Block you will need 1 yellow, 6 solid, 12 print and 18 green hexagons.

1. Referring to **Fig. 1**, center paper **hexagon** on wrong side of fabric **hexagon**, fold and finger press top seam allowance back over paper.

    Fig. 1

    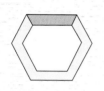

2. Working counter clockwise and mitering fabric at the corner, fold top left seam allowance back over paper. Stitching from corner to corner and only through the fabric, use a long stitch to hold seam allowances in place (**Fig. 2**).

    Fig. 2

    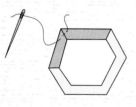

3. Referring to **Fig. 3** continue to fold and stitch seam allowances, taking a backstitch at each corner. Repeat for each **hexagon** in **Flower Block**.

    Fig. 3

    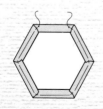

4. Matching right sides and corners, place yellow center and 1 solid **hexagon** together as shown in **Fig. 4**. Avoiding stitching through paper, and backstitching at beginning and end of seam, whipstitch edges together along one side. Open pieces flat (**Fig. 5**).

    Fig. 4

    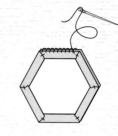

    Fig. 5

    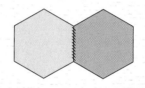

5. Continue adding solid **hexagons** one at a time until **Inner Ring** is completed. It is not necessary to knot and clip threads each time you reach the end of a **hexagon** side.

    Inner Ring

    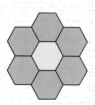

6. Add 12 print **hexagons** around **Inner Ring** until **Middle Ring** is completed.

Middle Ring

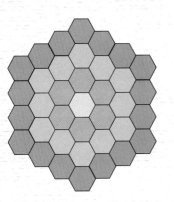

7. To make **Outer Ring** and complete **Flower Block**, add 18 green **hexagons** around **Middle Ring**. Make a total of 53 **Flower Blocks**.

Flower Block

8. Carefully remove papers from center **hexagon**, **Inner** and **Middle Rings**. Leave papers in **Outer Ring** until each **hexagon** in the ring is completely attached to another hexagon.
9. Repeat **Steps 1 - 3** for all white and remaining 24 green **hexagons**.

10. Referring to **Assembly Diagram**, page 42, arrange **Flower Blocks** in **vertical Rows**. Use white and green **hexagons** as connectors to join **Blocks** into **Rows** and to join **Rows** together to complete **Quilt Top**.

1. Follow **Quilting**, page 138, to mark, layer and quilt as desired. Our quilt is hand quilted with outline quilting $^1/_8$" from the seams of each **hexagon**.
2. Referring to **Quilt Top Diagram**, page 43, for placement, draw a cutting line around outside edge of quilt top. Stitch around edges of quilt $^1/_8$" inside drawn line. Trim edges of **Quilt Top**, backing, and batting along drawn line, being careful to only trim the protruding points of **hexagons**.
3. Cut a 28" square of binding fabric. Follow **Making Continuous Bias Strip Binding**, page 141, to make approximately $9^1/_2$ yards of 2"w bias binding.
4. Follow **Steps 1** and **2** of **Attaching Binding with Mitered Corners**, page 142, to pin binding to front of quilt, easing binding around curved edges. Sew binding to quilt until binding overlaps beginning end by approximately 2". Trim excess binding. Fold binding over to quilt backing and pin in place, covering stitching line. Blindstitch binding to backing.

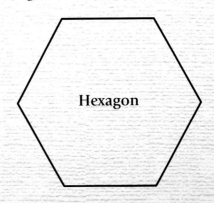

Assembly Diagram

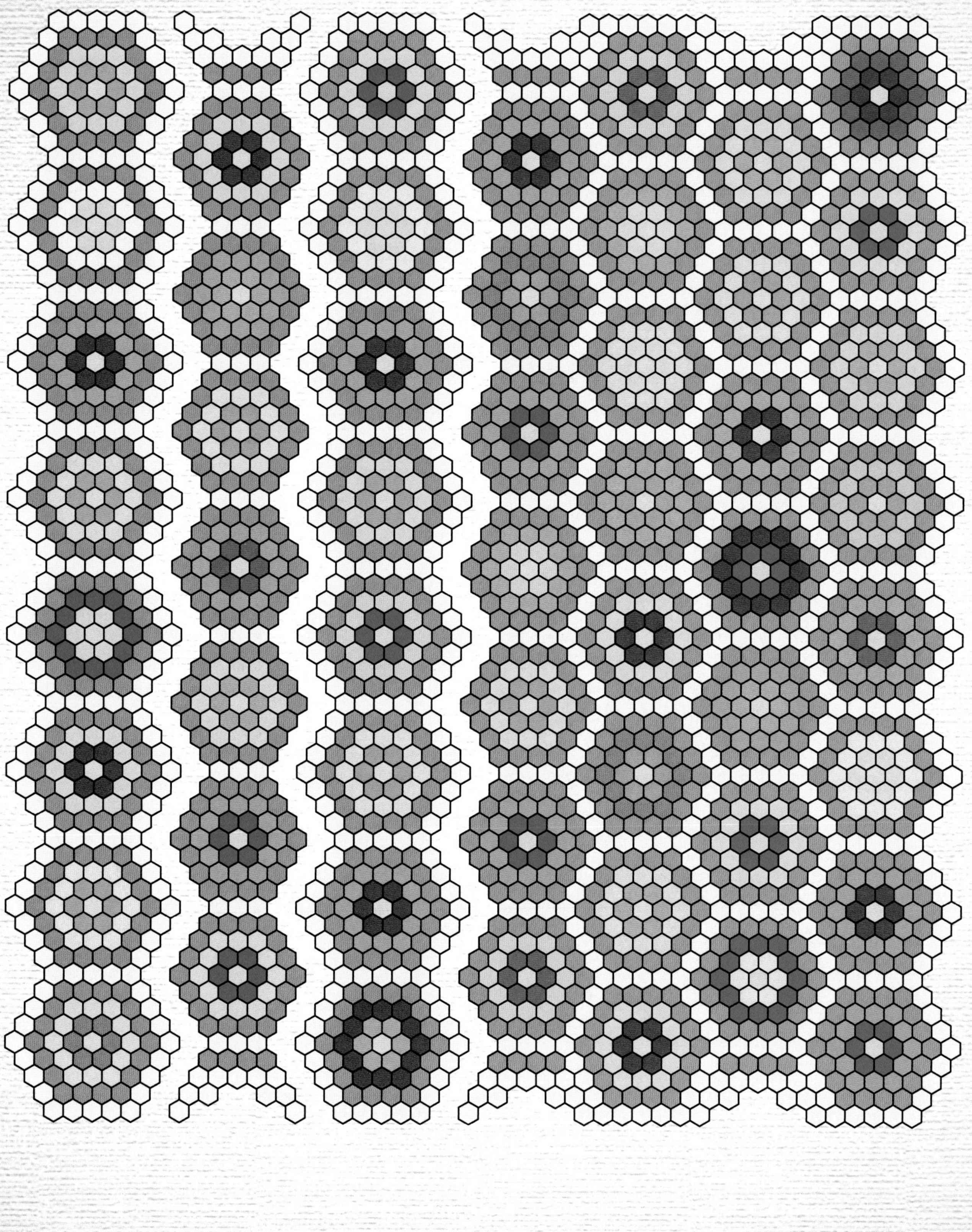

Cake Stand Quilt

A DELICIOUS MIX OF CHECKS AND PLAIDS

on a background of pink made this VINTAGE SCRAP

QUILT a treat for the eye. Shades of pink and salmon

were popular choices for quilts in the 1930's. The

plaid scraps may once have been men's shirts.

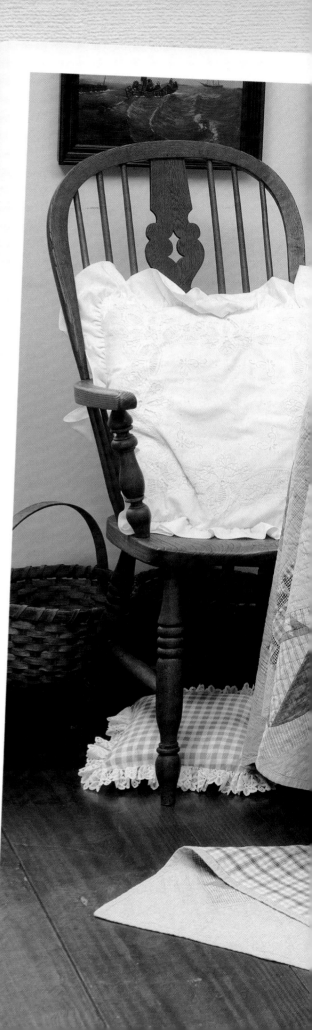

Cake Stand Quilt

SKILL LEVEL: 1 2 3 4 5

QUILT SIZE: 70" x 81$\frac{1}{2}$" (178 cm x 207 cm)

FINISHED BLOCK SIZE: 8$\frac{1}{8}$" x 8$\frac{1}{8}$" (21 cm x 21 cm)

PIECED BLOCKS: 42

Yardage Requirements

Yardage is based on 45"w fabric.

14" x 15" (36 cm x 38 cm) scrap of light
  print or solid for each block

8" x 13" (20 cm x 33 cm) scrap of dark
  print or solid for each block

$3^1/8$ yds (2.9 m) of pink solid

5 yds (4.6 m) of backing fabric

$^7/8$ yd (80 cm) of binding fabric

78" x 90" (198 cm x 229 cm) rectangle
  of batting

Cutting Out the Pieces

*Follow **Rotary Cutting**, page 133, to cut fabric.
All strips are cut across the width of the fabric
unless otherwise noted. All measurements include
a $^1/4$" seam allowance.*

From each light print or solid:
- Cut 3 **squares** $2^1/2$" x $2^1/2$" (**A**).
- Cut 1 **square** $2^1/8$" x $2^1/8$" (**B**).
- Cut 2 **rectangles** $2^1/8$" x $5^3/8$" (**C**).
- Cut 1 **square** $5^3/4$" x $5^3/4$". Cut **square** in half once diagonally to make 2 **triangles** (**D**). You will use 1 **D triangle**.
- Cut 1 **square** $4^1/8$" x $4^1/8$". Cut **square** in half once diagonally to make 2 **triangles** (**E**). You will use 1 **E triangle**.

From each dark print or solid:
- Cut 3 **squares** $2^1/2$" x $2^1/2$" (**A**).
- Cut 1 **square** $5^3/4$" x $5^3/4$". Cut **square** in half once diagonally to make 2 **triangles** (**D**). You will use 1 **D triangle**.
- Cut 1 **square** $2^1/2$" x $2^1/2$". Cut **square** in half once diagonally to make 2 **triangles** (**F**).

From pink solid:
- Cut 8 **strips** $8^5/8$"w. From these **strips**, cut 30 **setting squares** $8^5/8$" x $8^5/8$".
- Cut 2 **strips** $12^3/4$"w. From these **strips**, cut 6 **squares** $12^3/4$" x $12^3/4$". Cut each **square** in half twice diagonally to make 24 **setting triangles**. You will use 22 **setting triangles**.
- Cut 2 **squares** $6^5/8$" x $6^5/8$". Cut each **square** in half once diagonally to make 4 **corner triangles**.

Assembling the Quilt Top

*Follow **Piecing and Pressing**, page 135, to
assemble the quilt top.*

1. For each block, use 3 light and 3 dark **A's** and follow **Making Triangle-Squares**, page 136, to make 6 **Triangle-Squares**.
2. Refer to **Unit 1 Diagram** to sew 3 Triangle-Squares together.

Unit 1
(make 1)

3. Refer to **Unit 2 Diagram** to sew
    3 **Triangle-Squares** and 1 **B** together.

Unit 2
(make 1)

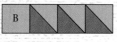

4. Refer to **Unit 3 Diagram** to sew 1 light
    and 1 dark **D** together.

Unit 3
(make 1)

5. Sew **Unit 1** then **Unit 2** to **Unit 3** to
    make **Unit 4**.

Unit 4
(make 1)

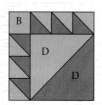

6. Referring to **Unit 5 Diagram** for
    orientation, sew 1 **F** and 1 **C** together to
    make 1 **Unit 5** and 1 **Unit 5 reversed**.

Unit 5   Unit 5 reversed
(make 1)   (make 1)

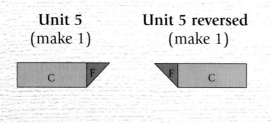

7. Sew **Unit 5** and **Unit 5 reversed** to
    Unit 4 to make **Unit 6**.

Unit 6
(make 1)

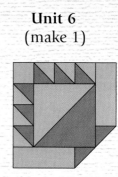

8. Sew **E** to **Unit 6** to complete **Cake
    Stand Block**.

Cake Stand Block

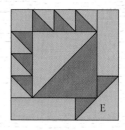

9. Repeat **Steps 1-8** to make 42 **Cake
    Stand Blocks**.
10. Referring to **Assembly Diagram**, sew
    corner triangles, **side triangles**, **squares**,
    and **Cake Stand Blocks** into diagonal
    Rows. Sew **Rows** together to complete
    Quilt Top.

Completing the Quilt

1. Follow **Quilting**, page 138, to mark,
    layer, and quilt as desired. Our quilt is
    hand quilted with diagonal lines, spaced
    approximately $3/4$" apart, across the
    entire quilt top.
2. Cut a 29" square of binding fabric.
    Follow **Binding**, page 141, to bind
    quilt using $2^1/2$"w bias binding with
    mitered corners.

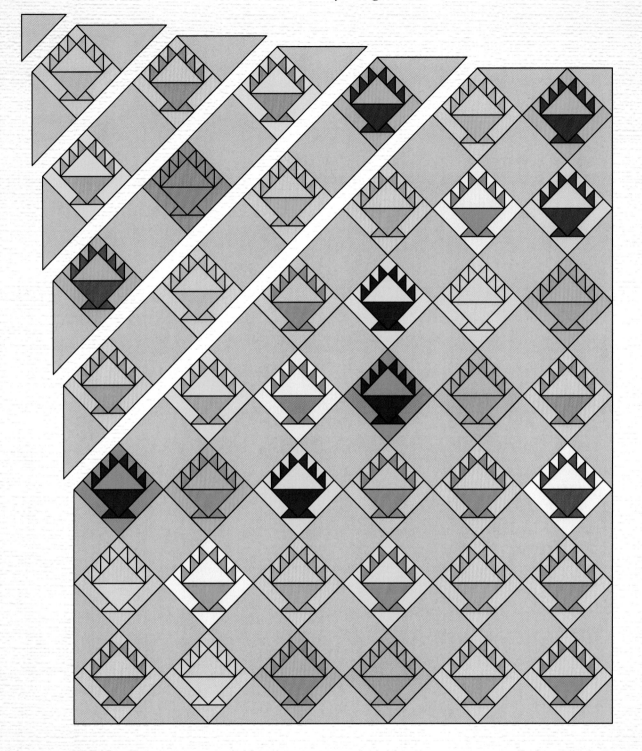

Maple Leaf

CREATED IN THE EARLY 1900'S, THIS MAPLE LEAF QUILT WAS FINISHED IN A HURRY. The quilter must have wanted to create a thing of beauty, because she was careful to use the same two fabrics for all her sashing pieces. However, her stitches averaged four-to-the-inch, and several leaf points were lost inside the seams. Given the LACK OF MODERN CONVENIENCES like central heat and other electrical appliances, the stitcher's speed is easy to understand — the quicker she sewed, the sooner she or someone else in her family could sleep under a warm quilt. It is fun to speculate which blocks, if not all, were CREATED BY CUTTING UP WORN SHIRTS OR DRESSES.

Maple Leaf Quilt

SKILL LEVEL: 1 2 3 4 5

QUILT SIZE: 64½" x 77" (164 cm x 196 cm)

FINISHED BLOCK SIZE: 10½" x 10½" (27 cm x 27 cm)

PIECED BLOCKS: 30

Yardage Requirements

Yardage is based on 45"w fabric.

  10" x 14" (25 cm x 36 cm) scrap of solid
   for **each** block
  10" x 14" (25 cm x 36 cm) scrap of print
   for **each** block
  10" x 20" (25 cm x 51 cm) rectangle of
   green solid
  $1^3/_8$ yds (1.3 m) of orange solid
  $4^3/_4$ yds (4.3 m) of muslin for backing
  72" x 85" (183 cm x 216 cm) rectangle
   of batting

Cutting Out the Pieces

*Follow **Rotary Cutting**, page 133, to cut fabric.
All strips are cut across the width of the fabric
unless otherwise noted. All measurements include
a $^1/_4$" seam allowance.*

From each scrap of solid:
  • Cut 2 **squares** $4^3/_8$" x $4^3/_8$" (**A**).
  • Cut 4 **squares** 4" x 4" (**B**).
From each scrap of print:
  • Cut 2 **squares** $4^3/_8$" x $4^3/_8$" (**A**).
  • Cut 1 **square** 4" x 4" (**B**).
  • Cut 2 **squares** $3^1/_4$" x $3^1/_4$" (**C**).
From green solid:
  • Cut 20 **sashing squares** $2^1/_2$" x $2^1/_2$".
From orange solid:
  • Cut 17 **strips** $2^1/_2$"w. From these **strips**,
   cut 49 **sashing strips** $2^1/_2$" x 11".
From muslin:
  • Cut 2 **backing rectangles** $36^1/_2$" x 85".

Assembling the Quilt Top

*Follow **Piecing and Pressing**, page 135, to
assemble the quilt top. For each block, you will
need 2 solid and 2 print A's, 1 print and 4 solid
B's, and 2 print C's.*

1. For each block, use 2 solid and 2 print
    A's and follow **Making Triangle-Squares**,
    page 136, to make 4 **Triangle-Squares**.
2. With right sides together and referring to
    Stem Unit Diagram, place 1 **C** on top of
    1 corner of a solid **B**. Stitch diagonally
    across **C**, trim excess fabric $^1/_4$" from
    stitching and press open. Repeat on
    opposite corner to complete **Stem Unit**.

Stem Unit
(make 1)

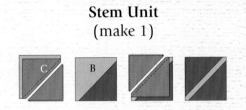

3. Sew 2 **Triangle-Squares** and 1 print **B**
    together to make **Unit 1**. Make **1 Unit 1**.

Unit 1
(make 1)

4. Sew 2 solid **B's** and 1 **Triangle-Square** together to make **Unit 2**. Make 1 **Unit 2**.

Unit 2
(make 1)

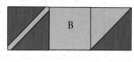

5. Sew **Stem Unit**, 1 solid **B**, and 1 **Triangle-Square** together to make **Unit 3**. Make 1 **Unit 3**.

Unit 3
(make 1)

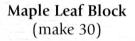

6. Sew **Units 1**, **2**, and **3** together to make **Maple Leaf Block**. Repeat **Steps 1-6** to make 30 **Maple Leaf Blocks**.

Maple Leaf Block
(make 30)

7. Sew 5 **Maple Leaf Blocks** and 4 **sashing strips** together to make **Row**. Make 6 **Rows**.

Row
(make 6)

8. Sew 5 **sashing strips** and 4 **sashing squares** together to make **Sashing Row**. Make 5 **Sashing Rows**.

Sashing Row
(make 5)

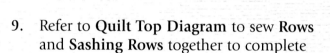

9. Refer to **Quilt Top Diagram** to sew **Rows** and **Sashing Rows** together to complete **Quilt Top**.

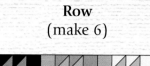

Completing the Quilt

1. Refer to **Quilting**, page 138, to prepare the backing, mark, layer, and quilt as desired. Our quilt is hand quilted with straight lines through the center of the sashings and in the blocks.
2. Leaving 2" of **batting** extending beyond edges of **Quilt Top and being careful not to cut backing**, trim **batting**. Leaving $2^1/_2$" of **backing** extending beyond edges of **batting**, trim **backing**.
3. Press raw edges of backing $1/_2$" to the wrong side.
4. To form a 2"w mock-binding, fold pressed edges of backing top and bottom to front of **Quilt Top**, covering raw edges of **Quilt Top**, and Blind Stitch to front of **Quilt Top**. Repeat for side edges to complete **Quilt**.

Happiness lies in the joy OF ACHIEVEMENT AND THE *thrill* OF CREATIVE EFFORT. ∽ Franklin Delano Roosevelt

Fruit Basket Quilt

NEARLY ONE HUNDRED YEARS OLD, THIS FRUIT BASKET

quilt has been both well-loved and carefully preserved. There are stains

and wear, but the quilt has never been laundered. The block is a variation

of the more common basket block styles. And although the quilt is signed

with embroidery, the signature raises more questions than it answers. One

corner bears the year "1908," while the other is initialed "FRF 11." We

can speculate that "F.R.F." was ELEVEN YEARS OLD when she completed

the quilt, but we can never be quite certain.

If you decide to LABEL YOUR OWN FABRIC CREATIONS for posterity,

please include your full name, the complete date, and where you live.

Future quilt lovers will be very appreciative of your efforts!

Fruit Basket Quilt

SKILL LEVEL: 1 2 3 4 5

QUILT SIZE: 75 1/4" x 87 5/8" (191 cm x 223 cm)

FINISHED BLOCK SIZE: 8 3/4" x 8 3/4" (22 cm x 22 cm)

PIECED BLOCKS: 42

Yardage Requirements

Yardage is based on 45"w fabric.

5$^1/_4$ yds (4.8 m) **total** of assorted light prints

2$^1/_4$ yds (2 m) **total** of assorted dark prints or solids

$^3/_4$ yd (69 cm) **total** of assorted red prints or solids

3$^1/_8$ yds (2.9 m) of blue solid

5$^1/_4$ yds (4.8 m) of backing fabric

$^7/_8$ yd (80 cm) of binding fabric

84" x 96" (213 cm x 244 cm) rectangle of batting

Cutting Out the Pieces

*Follow **Rotary Cutting**, page 133, to cut fabric. All strips are cut across the width of the fabric unless otherwise noted. All measurements include a $^1/_4$" seam allowance.*

For each block, from assorted light prints:

- Cut 6 **squares** 2$^5/_8$" x 2$^5/_8$". Cut each **square** in half once diagonally to make 12 **triangles (A)**. You will use 11 **A triangles**.
- Cut 1 **square** 2$^1/_4$" x 2$^1/_4$" **(B)**.
- Cut 1 **square** 4$^3/_8$" x 4$^3/_8$". Cut **square** in half once diagonally to make 2 **triangles (C)**.
- Cut 2 **rectangles** 2$^1/_4$" x 5$^3/_4$" **(D)**.

For each block, from assorted dark prints or solids:

- Cut 4 **squares** 2$^5/_8$" x 2$^5/_8$". Cut each **square** in half once diagonally to make 8 **triangles (E)**.
- Cut 1 **square** 4$^3/_8$" x 4$^3/_8$". Cut **square** in half once diagonally to make 2 **triangles (F)**. You will use 1 **F triangle**.

For each block, from assorted red prints or solids:

- Cut 3 **squares** 2$^5/_8$" x 2$^5/_8$". Cut each **square** in half once diagonally to make 6 **triangles (G)**. You will use 5 **G triangles**.

From blue solid:

- Cut 8 **strips** 9$^1/_4$"w. From these **strips**, cut 30 **setting squares** 9$^1/_4$" x 9$^1/_4$".
- Cut 2 **strips** 13$^5/_8$"w. From these **strips**, cut 6 **squares** 13$^5/_8$" x 13$^5/_8$". Cut each **square** in half twice diagonally to make 24 **setting triangles**. You will use 22 **setting triangles**.
- Cut 2 **squares** 7$^1/_8$" x 7$^1/_8$". Cut each **square** in half once diagonally to make 4 **corner triangles**.

Assembling the Quilt Top

*Follow **Piecing and Pressing**, page 135, to assemble the quilt top.*

1. For each block, sew 6 **A** and 6 **E triangles** together to make 6 **Handle Units**. Repeat using 3 **A** and 3 **G triangles** to make 3 **Fruit Units**.

Handle Unit	Fruit Unit
(make 6)	(make 3)

2. Refer to **Unit 1 Diagram** to sew 3 **Handle Units** together.

Unit 1
(make 1)

3. Refer to **Unit 2 Diagram** to sew 3 **Handle Units** and **1 B** together.

Unit 2
(make 1)

4. Refer to **Unit 3 Diagram** to sew **A** and **G** **triangles** to **Fruit Units** and to sew **Fruit Units** together to make **Unit 3**.

Unit 3
(make 1)

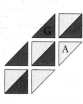

5. Sew **C** then **F** to **Unit 3** to make **Unit 4**.

Unit 4
(make 1)

6. Sew **Unit 1**, then **Unit 2** to **Unit 4** to make **Unit 5**.

Unit 5
(make 1)

7. Referring to **Unit 6 Diagrams** for orientation, sew **1 E** and **1 D** together to make **Unit 6**. Sew **1 E** and **1 D** together to make **Unit 6 reversed**.

Unit 6   **Unit 6 reversed**
(make 1)   (make 1)

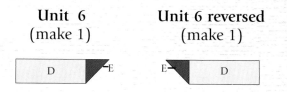

8. Sew **Unit 6** and **Unit 6 reversed** to **Unit 5** to make **Unit 7**.

Unit 7
(make 1)

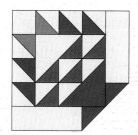

9. Sew **C** to **Unit 7** to complete **Fruit Basket Block**.

Fruit Basket Block

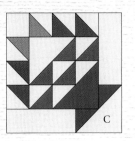

10. Repeat **Steps 1-9** to make 42 **Fruit Basket Blocks**.
11. Referring to **Assembly Diagram**, sew **corner triangles**, **side triangles**, **squares**, and **Fruit Basket Blocks** into diagonal **Rows**. Sew **Rows** together to complete **Quilt Top**.

1. Follow **Quilting**, page 138, to mark, layer, and quilt as desired. Our quilt is hand quilted with a $^3/_4$" grid pattern in the blue squares and triangles. There are evenly spaced pairs of parallel lines quilted in the basket blocks.
2. Cut a 27" **square** of binding fabric. Follow **Binding**, page 141, to bind quilt using $2^1/_2$"w bias binding with mitered corners.

Assembly Diagram

Bear's Paw Quilt

THIS CHARMING OLD QUILT HAS A FEW PATCHES of fabric that could have been produced prior to 1880. The CAREFULLY MATCHED SEAMS and ATTENTION TO DETAIL show the counterpane to be a LABOR OF LOVE, and its creator may very well have used every scrap of fabric she owned. What leads us to this conclusion? Two of the white patches may have come from the end of a fabric bolt, for with careful examination, the words "COCHECO MANUFACTURING CO." can be seen.

Bear's Paw Quilt

SKILL LEVEL: 1 2 **3** 4 5

QUILT SIZE: 79 ½" x 93" (202 cm x 236 cm)

BLOCK SIZE: 14" x 14" (36 cm x 36 cm)

PIECED BLOCKS: 20

· CLASSIC ·

Yardage Requirements

Yardage is based on 45"w fabric.

2¹/₂ yds (2.3 m) of cream solid

3 yds (2.7 m) **total** of assorted medium
  and dark prints

1¹/₈ yds (1 m) **total** of assorted
  light prints

¹/₄ yd (23 cm) **total** of assorted red prints

¹/₂ yd (46 cm) of red print

2¹/₂ yds (2.3 m) of blue with small
  polka dots

³/₈ yd (34 cm) of blue with medium
  polka dots

5³/₄ yds (5.3 m) of backing fabric

1 yd (91 cm) of binding fabric

87" x 100¹/₂" (221 cm x 255 cm)
  rectangle of batting

Cutting Out the Pieces

*Follow **Rotary Cutting**, page 133, to cut fabric.
All strips are cut across the width of the fabric
unless otherwise noted. All measurements include
a ¹/₄" seam allowance.*

From assorted medium and dark prints:
  • Cut 400 **squares** 2¹/₂" x 2¹/₂" (**A**).
  • Cut 160 **squares** 2⁷/₈" x 2⁷/₈" (**C**).
From red print:
  • Cut 20 **border squares** 5" x 5" (**B**).
From assorted light prints:
  • Cut 160 **squares** 2⁷/₈" x 2⁷/₈" (**C**).
From cream solid:
  • Cut 80 **rectangles** 2¹/₂" x 6¹/₂" (**D**).
  • Cut 41 **border strips** 2" x 14¹/₂" (**E**).
From assorted red prints:
  • Cut 20 **center squares** 2¹/₂" x 2¹/₂" (**F**).
From blue with small polka dots:
  • Cut 82 **border strips** 2" x 14¹/₂" (**E**).
From blue with medium polka dots:
  • Cut 1 **top** and 1 **bottom border**
    2¹/₂" x 79", piecing as necessary.

Assembling the Quilt Top

*This quilt's scrappy look comes from random
placement of the light, medium and dark
C squares. Follow **Piecing and Pressing**,
page 135, to assemble the quilt top.*

1. Using 1 light and 1 medium or dark
    C square, follow **Making Triangle-
    Squares**, page 136, to make 320
    Triangle-Squares.
2. For each block, sew 2 **Triangle-Squares**
    together to make **Unit 1**. Make 4 **Unit
    1's**. Sew 2 **Triangle-Squares** together to
    make **Unit 2**. Make 4 **Unit 2's**.

Unit 1
(make 4)

Unit 2
(make 4)

3. Sew 1 **A** and **Unit 1** together to make
    Unit 3. Make 4 **Unit 3's**.

Unit 3
(make 4)

4. Sew 4 **A's** together to make **Unit 4**. Make 4 **Unit 4's**.

Unit 4
(make 4)

5. Sew 1 **Unit 2** and 1 **Unit 4** together to make **Unit 5**. Make 4 **Unit 5's**.

Unit 5
(make 4)

6. Sew 1 **Unit 3** and 1 **Unit 5** together to make **Unit 6**. Make 4 **Unit 6's**.

Unit 6
(make 4)

7. Sew 2 **Unit 6's** and 1 **D** together to make **Unit 7**. Make 2 **Unit 7's**.

Unit 7
(make 2)

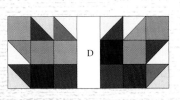

8. Sew 2 **D's** and 1 **F** together to make **Unit 8**.

Unit 8

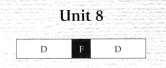

9. Sew 2 **Unit 7's** and **Unit 8** together to make **Bear Paw Block**.

Bear Paw Block

10. Repeat **Steps 2-9** to make a total of 20 **Bear Paw Blocks**.

11. Sew 1 cream and 2 blue **border strips (E)** together to make **Border Unit**. Make 41 **Border Units**.

Border Unit
(make 41)

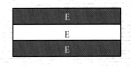

12. Sew 4 **Blocks** and 5 **Border Unit's** together to make **Row**. Make 5 **Rows**.

Row
(make 5)

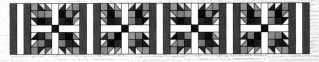

13. Sew 5 **border squares (B)** and 4 **Border Unit's** together to make a **Border Row**. Make 4 **Border Rows**.

Border Row
(make 4)

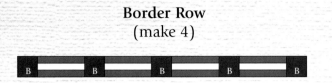

14. Refer to **Quilt Top Diagram**, to sew 5 **Rows** and 4 **Border Rows** together. Add **top**, then **bottom borders** to complete piecing the **Quilt Top**.

1. Follow **Quilting**, page 138, to mark, layer, and quilt as desired. Our quilt is hand quilted with cross hatching in the blocks and diagonal lines in the sashings and borders.

2. Cut a 31" square of binding fabric. Follow **Binding**, page 141, to bind quilt using $2^1/_2$"w bias binding with mitered corners.

Quilt Top Diagram

FOR OUR QUILT, WE REPRODUCED A FEW BLOCKS OF THE

CLASSIC QUILT IN SHADES OF RED AND TAN. We added hearts to the setting squares in the sashing —

another way to show your affection for all things quilted. Bear's Paw quilts are also popular gifts for

men when sewn with fabrics in masculine hues.

Bear's Paw Quilt

SKILL LEVEL: 1 2 3 4 5

QUILT SIZE: 42$^1/_2$" x 61" (108 cm x 155 cm)

FINISHED BLOCK SIZE: 14" x 14" (36 cm x 36 cm)

PIECED BLOCKS: 6

Yardage Requirements

Yardage is based on 45"w fabric.

$^3/_4$ yd (69 cm) **total** of assorted tan prints

1 yd (91 cm) **total** of assorted red prints

2 yds (1.8 m) **total** of assorted cream prints

1$^1/_8$ yds (1 m) of red print for borders

3 yds (2.7 m) of backing fabric

$^3/_4$ yd (69 cm) of binding fabric

51" x 69" (130 cm x 175 cm) rectangle of batting

You will also need:

Tan embroidery floss

Paper-backed fusible web

Cutting Out the Pieces

Follow **Rotary Cutting**, page 133, to cut fabric. All strips are cut across the width of the fabric unless otherwise noted. All measurements include a $^1/_4$" seam allowance. Follow **Preparing Fusible Appliqué**, page 137, to use heart pattern, page 70.

From assorted tan prints:

- Cut 72 **squares** 2$^1/_2$" x 2$^1/_2$" **(A)**. Cut 8 of the same fabric and 4 of assorted fabrics for each block.
- Cut 12 **border squares** 5" x 5" **(B)**.

From assorted cream prints:
- Cut 48 **squares** $2^7/8$" x $2^7/8$" (**C**).
- Cut 24 **rectangles** $2^1/2$" x $6^1/2$" (**D**).
- Cut 17 **border strips** 2" x $14^1/2$" (**E**).

From assorted red prints:
- Cut 48 **squares** $2^7/8$" x $2^7/8$" (**C**).
- Cut 48 **squares** $2^1/2$" x $2^1/2$" (**A**).
- Cut 12 **hearts**.

From red print for borders:
- Cut 34 **border strips** 2" x $14^1/2$" (**E**).
- Cut 6 **center squares** $2^1/2$" x $2^1/2$" (**F**).

Assembling the Quilt Top

Follow **Piecing and Pressing**, *page 135, to assemble the quilt top.*

1. For each block, using cream and red **C's**, follow **Making Triangle-Squares**, page 136, to make 96 **Triangle-Squares**.
2. Follow **Steps 2-9** of **Bear's Paw Quilt**, page 65, to make 6 **Bear's Paw Blocks**.

Heart

3. Sew 1 cream and 2 red **border strips** (**E**) together to make **Border Unit**. Make 17 **Border Units**.
4. Sew 2 **Blocks** and 3 **Border Units** together to make **Row**. Make 3 **Rows**.
5. Sew 3 **border squares** and 2 **Border Units** together to make **Border Row**. Make 4 **Border Rows**.
6. Refer to **Quilt Top Diagram**, to sew 3 **Rows** and 4 **Border Rows** together to complete piecing the **Quilt Top**.
7. Following **Fusible Appliqué**, page 137, center, then fuse 1 heart to each border square. Blanket Stitch, page 144, around hearts using 3 strands of tan floss.

Quilt Top Diagram

Completing the Quilt

1. Follow **Quilting**, page 138, to mark, layer, and quilt as desired. Our quilt is machine quilted with cross-hatching over the entire quilt top.

2. Cut a 24" square of binding fabric. Follow **Binding**, page 141, to bind quilt using 2$\frac{1}{2}$"w bias binding with mitered corners.

Basket Quilt

THIS QUILT MAY HAVE BEEN **FINISHED AT A QUILTING BEE,** the fabrics coming from OLD DRESSES — a result of necessity as well as sentiment. Most of the BLOCKS ARE SIGNED BY THEIR CREATORS IN INK, a common way to personalize a quilt in the 1800's. The ink bled, so several of the blocks were signed a second time. However, both inks were affected over time, the first completely eating away the fabric, and the second wearing away until only ONE DATE CAN BE DISCERNED: JUNE 26, 1873. Today, there are

several brands of permanent, acid-free ink pens that quilters can use to document their quilts and thus avoid damaging the fabric.

Basket Quilt

SKILL LEVEL: 1 2 3 4 5

QUILT SIZE: 75" x 88" (191 cm x 224 cm)

FINISHED BLOCK SIZE: 10" x 10" (25 cm x 25 cm)

PIECED BLOCKS: 30

· CLASSIC ·

Yardage Requirements

Yardage is based on 45"w fabric.

- 2$\frac{1}{4}$ yds (2 m) of tan solid
- 9" x 12" (23 cm x 30 cm) scrap of fabric No. 1 for each block
- 7" x 10" (18 cm x 25 cm) scrap of fabric No. 2 for each block
- 3 yds (2.7 m) of brown solid
- 2$\frac{3}{8}$ yds (2.2 m) of green print
- 5$\frac{3}{8}$ yds (4.9 m) of backing fabric
- $\frac{7}{8}$ yd (80 cm) of binding fabric
- 83" x 96" (211 cm x 244 cm) rectangle of batting

Cutting Out the Pieces

*Follow **Rotary Cutting**, page 133, to cut fabric. All strips are cut across the width of the fabric unless otherwise noted. All measurements include a $\frac{1}{4}$" seam allowance.*

From tan solid:
- Cut 4 **strips** 8$\frac{7}{8}$"w. From these **strips**, cut 15 **squares** 8$\frac{7}{8}$" x 8$\frac{7}{8}$". Cut each **square** in half once diagonally to make 30 **triangles (A)**.
- Cut 2 **strips** 4$\frac{7}{8}$"w. From these **strips**, cut 15 **squares** 4$\frac{7}{8}$" x 4$\frac{7}{8}$". Cut each **square** in half once diagonally to make 30 **triangles (B)**.
- Cut 10 **strips** 2$\frac{1}{2}$"w. From these **strips**, cut 60 **rectangles** 2$\frac{1}{2}$" x 6$\frac{1}{2}$" **(C)**.

From each fabric No. 1:
- Cut 6 **squares** 2$\frac{7}{8}$" x 2$\frac{7}{8}$" **(D)**. Cut 3 of the D squares in half once diagonally to make 6 **triangles (E)**.
- Cut 1 **basket handle**.

From each fabric No. 2:
- Cut 3 **squares** 2$\frac{7}{8}$" x 2$\frac{7}{8}$" **(D)**.
- Cut 1 **square** 2$\frac{1}{2}$" x 2$\frac{1}{2}$" **(F)**.

From brown solid:
- Cut 2 *lengthwise* **top** and **bottom inner borders** 2$\frac{1}{2}$" x 74$\frac{1}{2}$".
- Cut 2 *lengthwise* **side inner borders** 2$\frac{1}{2}$" x 75$\frac{1}{2}$".
- Cut 2 *lengthwise* **top** and **bottom outer borders** 2$\frac{1}{2}$" x 74$\frac{1}{2}$".
- Cut 2 *lengthwise* **side outer borders** 2$\frac{1}{2}$" x 75$\frac{1}{2}$".
- Cut 8 *lengthwise* **long sashing strips** 1$\frac{1}{2}$" x 75$\frac{1}{2}$".
- Cut 50 **short sashing strips** 1$\frac{1}{2}$" x 10$\frac{1}{2}$".

From green print:
- Cut 2 *lengthwise* **top** and **bottom middle borders** 2$\frac{1}{2}$" x 74$\frac{1}{2}$".
- Cut 2 *lengthwise* **side middle borders** 2$\frac{1}{2}$" x 75$\frac{1}{2}$".
- Cut 4 *lengthwise* **long sashing strips** 1$\frac{1}{2}$" x 75$\frac{1}{2}$".
- Cut 25 **short sashing strips** 1$\frac{1}{2}$" x 10$\frac{1}{2}$".

Assembling the Quilt Top

*Follow **Piecing and Pressing**, page 135, to assemble the quilt top.*

1. For each block, use 3 **No. 1** and 3 **No. 2 D's** and follow **Making Triangle-Squares**, page 136, to make 6 **Triangle-Squares**. Discard 1 **Triangle-Square**.

2. Refer to **Unit 1 Diagram** to sew 5 **Triangle-Squares**, 4 **E**'s, and **1 F** into **rows**. Sew **rows** together to make **Unit 1**.

Unit 1
(make 1)

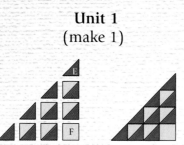

3. Referring to **Unit 2 Diagram** for orientation, sew 1 **E** and 1 **C** together to make 1 **Unit 2** and 1 **Unit 2 reversed**.

Unit 2	**Unit 2 reversed**
(make 1)	(make 1)

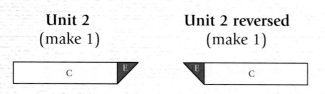

4. Refer to **Unit 3 Diagram** to sew **Unit 2**, **Unit 2 reversed** and 1 **B** to **Unit 1** to make **Unit 3**.

Unit 3
(make 1)

5. Referring to **Block Diagram** for placement and following **Needleturn Appliqué**, page 137, appliqué 1 basket handle to **A** to make **Unit 4**.

Unit 4
(make 1)

6. Sew **Unit's 3** and **4** together to complete **Basket Block**. Repeat **Steps 1-6** to make a total of 30 **Basket Blocks**.

Basket Block
(make 30)

7. Sew 1 green and 2 brown **short sashing strips** together to make a **Short Sashing Unit**. Make 25 **Short Sashing Units**.

Short Sashing Unit
(make 25)

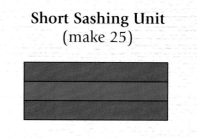

8. Sew 1 green and 2 brown **long sashing strips** together to make a **Long Sashing Unit**. Make 4 **Long Sashing Units**.

9. Refer to **Assembly Diagram** to sew 6 **Basket Blocks** and 5 **Short Sashing Units** into **Vertical Rows**. Make 5 **Vertical Rows**. Keeping horizontal sashing strips aligned, sew **Rows** together with **Long Sashing Units** to complete center section of **Quilt Top**.

10. Referring to **Assembly Diagram**, sew **inner**, **middle**, and **outer Side Borders** together. Repeat for remaining **inner**, **middle**, and **outer Side Borders**. Sew **Side Borders** to center section of **Quilt Top**.

11. Sew **inner**, **middle**, and **outer Top Borders** together. Repeat for **Bottom Border**. Sew **Top and Bottom Borders** to center section of **Quilt Top**.

Completing the Quilt

2. Cut a 30" square of binding fabric. Follow **Binding**, page 141, to bind quilt using $2^1/_2$"w bias binding with slightly rounded corners.

1. Follow **Quilting**, page 138, to mark, layer, and quilt as desired. Our quilt was hand quilted with overlapping circles in the blocks, diagonal lines in the sashings, and a fan pattern in the borders.

Assembly Diagram

TO UPDATE THIS BELOVED OLD PATTERN, WE CHOSE MODERN FABRICS IN HUES GUARANTEED TO RETAIN THE FEEL OF AN ANTIQUE. In fact, these new fabrics are reproductions of popular Depression-era prints. Look closely, you may spot look-alikes of old family favorites stitched into these colorful new blocks.

Basket Quilt

SKILL LEVEL: 1 2 3 4 5

QUILT SIZE: 75" x 88" (191 cm x 224 cm)

FINISHED BLOCK SIZE: 10" x 10" (25 cm x 25 cm)

PIECED BLOCKS: 30

Yardage Requirements

Yardage is based on 45"w fabric.

$2^1/4$ yds (2 m) of white solid

9" x 12" (23 cm x 30 cm) scrap of dark print for **each** block

7" x 10" (18 cm x 25 cm) scrap of light print for **each** block

3 yds (2.7 m) of red print

$2^3/8$ yds (2.2 m) of green print

$5^3/8$ yds (4.9 m) of backing fabric

$7/8$ yd (80 cm) of binding fabric

83" x 96" (211 cm x 244 cm) rectangle of batting

Cutting Out the Pieces

Follow **Rotary Cutting**, page 133, to cut fabric. All strips are cut across the width of the fabric unless otherwise noted. All measurements include a $1/4$" seam allowance.

From white solid:

- Cut 4 **strips** $8^7/8$"w. From these **strips**, cut 15 **squares** $8^7/8$" x $8^7/8$". Cut each **square** in half once diagonally to make 30 **triangles (A)**.
- Cut 2 **strips** $4^7/8$"w. From these **strips**, cut 15 **squares** $4^7/8$" x $4^7/8$". Cut each **square** in half once diagonally to make 30 **triangles (B)**.
- Cut 10 **strips** $2^1/2$"w. From these **strips**, cut 60 **rectangles** $2^1/2$" x $6^1/2$" **(C)**.

From each dark print:
- Cut 6 **squares** $2^7/8$" x $2^7/8$" (**D**). Cut 3 of the **D** squares in half once diagonally to make 6 **triangles** (**E**).
- Cut 1 **basket handle**.

From each light print:
- Cut 3 **squares** $2^7/8$" x $2^7/8$" (**D**).
- Cut 1 **square** $2^1/2$" x $2^1/2$" (**F**).

From red print:
- Cut 2 *lengthwise* **top** and **bottom inner borders** $2^1/2$" x $74^1/2$".
- Cut 2 *lengthwise* **side inner borders** $2^1/2$" x $75^1/2$".
- Cut 2 *lengthwise* **top** and **bottom outer borders** $2^1/2$" x $74^1/2$".
- Cut 2 *lengthwise* **side outer borders** $2^1/2$" x $75^1/2$".
- Cut 8 *lengthwise* **long sashing strips** $1^1/2$" x $75^1/2$".
- Cut 50 **short sashing strips** $1^1/2$" x $10^1/2$".

From green print:
- Cut 2 *lengthwise* **top and bottom middle borders** $2^1/2$" x $74^1/2$".
- Cut 2 *lengthwise* **side middle borders** $2^1/2$" x $75^1/2$".
- Cut 4 *lengthwise* **long sashing strips** $1^1/2$" x $75^1/2$".
- Cut 25 **short sashing strips** $1^1/2$" x $10^1/2$".

Assembling the Quilt Top

Follow **Piecing and Pressing**, *page 135, and* **Steps 1-11** *of Basket Quilt, page 76, to assemble the quilt top.*

Completing the Quilt

1. Follow **Quilting**, page 138, to mark, layer, and quilt as desired. Our quilt is machine quilted in the ditch around the baskets and in the sashings. A meandering pattern is quilted in the block backgrounds.
2. Cut a 30" square of binding fabric. Follow **Binding**, page 141, to bind quilt using $2^1/2$"w bias binding with mitered corners.

Quilt Top Diagram

English Ivy Quilt

ALSO KNOWN AS **CAROLINA LILY** OR **TREE OF LIFE**, the block

that forms this antique quilt has been traced to the early 1800's. The

salmon pink setting squares hint that this particular quilt was sewn in

the 1920's or 1930's, at a time when "COLONIAL" decorating was in

vogue. English Ivy is not a quilt that most beginning stitchers would

attempt, but if its GARDEN THEME and INTRIGUING SHAPE should appeal

to a novice quilter, then she will find it well worth her

time to make a few practice blocks before creating

her own ROMANTIC QUILT of PATCHWORK IVY.

English Ivy Quilt

SKILL LEVEL: 1 2 3 4 5

QUILT SIZE: $90\frac{3}{4}$" x 79" (231 cm x 200 cm)

FINISHED BLOCK SIZE: $8\frac{1}{4}$" x $8\frac{1}{4}$" (21 cm x 21 cm)

PIECED BLOCKS: 42

• CLASSIC •

Yardage Requirements

Yardage is based on 45"w fabric.

   8" x 10" (20 cm x 25 cm) scrap of 42
     prints or solids
   $2^7/8$ yds (2.6 m) of white solid
   $7/8$ yd (80 cm) **total** of assorted
     gold prints
   $3^1/4$ yds (2.9 m) of pink solid
   $2^1/2$ yds (2.3 m) of white print for borders
   $5^1/2$ yds (5 m) of backing fabric
   $7/8$ yd (80 cm) of binding fabric
   98" x 86" (218 cm x 101 cm) rectangle
     of batting

Cutting out the Pieces

*Follow **Rotary Cutting**, page 133, to cut fabric. All strips are cut across the width of the fabric unless otherwise noted. All measurements include a $^1/4$" seam allowance.*

From each scrap of print or solid:

- Cut 4 **squares** $2^1/4$" x $2^1/4$" (**A**).
- Cut 1 **square** $3^5/8$" x $3^5/8$". Cut **square** in half once diagonally to make 2 **triangles** (**B**).
- Cut 1 **square** $3^1/4$" x $3^1/4$" (**C**).
- Cut 1 **square** $1^7/8$" x $1^7/8$" (**D**).

From white solid:
- Cut 12 **strips** $2^1/_4$"w. From these **strips**, cut 210 **squares** $2^1/_4$" x $2^1/_4$" (**A**). Cut 42 **squares** in half once diagonally to make 84 **triangles** (**E**).
- Cut 6 **strips** 5"w. From these **strips**, cut 42 **squares** 5" x 5". Cut each **square** in half once diagonally to make 84 **triangles** (**F**).
- Cut 9 **strips** 4"w. From these **strips**, cut 84 **squares** 4" x 4" (**G**).

From assorted gold prints:
- Cut 42 **squares** $4^5/_8$" x $4^5/_8$" (**H**).

From pink solid:
- Cut 8 **strips** $8^3/_4$"w. From these **strips**, cut 30 **setting squares** $8^3/_4$" x $8^3/_4$".
- Cut 1 **strip** $6^3/_4$"w. From this **strip**, cut 2 **squares** $6^3/_4$" x $6^3/_4$". Cut each **square** in half once diagonally to make 4 **corner triangles**.
- Cut 2 **strips** 13"w. From these **strips**, cut 6 **squares** 13" x 13". Cut each **square** in half twice diagonally to make 24 **setting triangles** (you will use 22).
- Cut 1 **strip** $4^1/_2$"w. From this **strip**, cut 4 **border squares** $4^1/_2$" x $4^1/_2$".

From white print for borders:
- Cut 2 **side borders** $4^1/_2$" x $74^1/_2$".
- Cut 2 **top** and **bottom borders** $4^1/_2$" x $86^1/_4$".

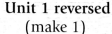

Assembling the Quilt Top

*Follow **Piecing and Pressing**, page 135, to assemble the quilt top. For **each block**, you will need 8 **Triangle-Squares**, 2 B's, 1 C, and 1 D from the same print fabric. From white fabric you will need 2 E's, 2 F's, and 2 G's. From gold fabric you will need 1 H. **Note:** Setting and corner triangles are cut slightly larger than needed. Square **Quilt Top** as needed after assembling.*

1. For each block, use white and print **A's** and follow **Making Triangle-Squares**, page 136, to make 8 **Triangle-Squares**.
2. Sew 2 **Triangle-Squares** and 1 **E** together to make 1 **Unit 1** and 1 **Unit 1 reversed**.

Unit 1   **Unit 1 reversed**
(make 1)   (make 1)

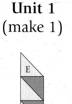

3. Sew 1 **B** to **Unit 1** and **Unit 1 reversed**, then add 1 **F** to make **Unit 2** and **Unit 2 reversed**.

Unit 2   **Unit 2 reversed**
(make 1)   (make 1)

4. Sew 2 **Triangle-Squares** and 1 **D** together to make 1 **Unit 3**.

Unit 3
(make 1)

5. Sew 2 **Triangle-Squares** and 1 **C** together to make 1 **Unit 4**.

Unit 4
(make 1)

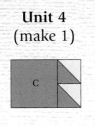

6. Sew **Unit 3** and **Unit 4** together to make **Unit 5**.

Unit 5
(make 1)

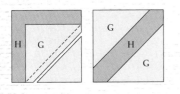

7. With right sides together and referring to **Unit 6 Diagram**, place 1 **G** on top of 1 corner of **H**. Stitch diagonally across **G**; trim excess fabric ¹/₄" from stitching and press open. Repeat on opposite corner to complete **Unit 6**.

Unit 6
(make 1)

8. Sew **Unit 2** and **Unit 5** together to make **Unit 7**.

Unit 7
(make 1)

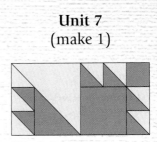

9. Sew **Unit 2 reversed** and **Unit 6** together to make **Unit 8**.

Unit 8
(make 1)

10. Sew **Unit 7** and **Unit 8** together to make **English Ivy Block**.

English Ivy Block
(make 1)

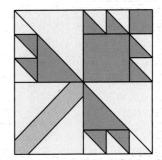

11. Repeat **Steps 1-10** to make a total of 42 **English Ivy Blocks**.
12. Referring to **Assembly Diagram**, sew **corner triangles**, **side triangles**, **squares**, and **English Ivy Blocks** into diagonal **Rows**. Sew **Rows** together to make center section of **Quilt Top**.
13. Measure center width of **Quilt Top** and trim **top** and **bottom borders** to determined measurement. Sew 1 **border corner** to each end of **top** and **bottom borders**.
14. Measure center length of **Quilt Top** and trim **side borders** to determined measurement. Sew **side**, then **top** and **bottom borders** to **Quilt Top**.

1. Follow **Quilting**, page 138, to mark, layer, and quilt as desired. Our quilt was hand quilted with parallel vertical lines through the pieced blocks. The setting squares are quilted with parallel vertical and diagonal lines. The borders are quilted with parallel diagonal lines.
2. Cut a 31" square of binding fabric. Follow **Binding**, page 141, to bind quilt using $2^{1}/_{2}$"w bias binding with mitered corners.

Assembly Diagram

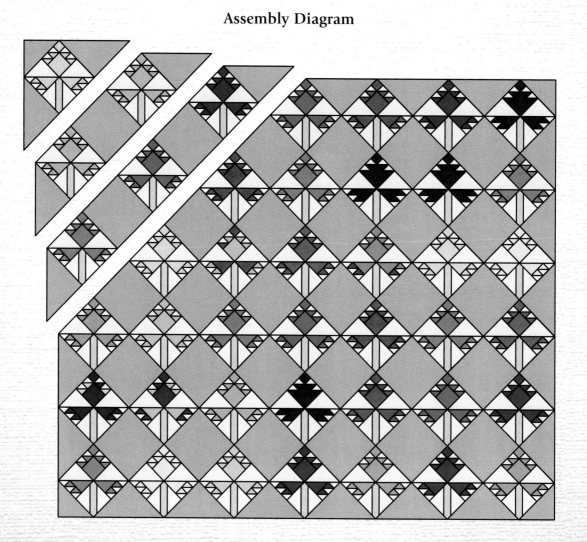

WE SHOULD **HAVE NOTHING** IN **OUR HOUSES,**

WHICH WE DID NOT EITHER **KNOW TO BE USEFUL** OR

believe TO BE *beautiful.*

∞ **William Morris,** 1880

IT'S EXCITING TO SEE WHAT MODERN FABRIC COLORS

CAN DO WHEN STITCHED TOGETHER TO FORM CLASSIC QUILT BLOCKS. On this new quilt, a soft celery green border and alternating squares of light sage form a restful backdrop for English Ivy leaves in pastel shades. Although true English ivy is considered an evergreen vine in most gardens, this pattern would look just as appealing sewn with autumn colors from your scrap bag.

English Ivy Quilt

SKILL LEVEL: 1 2 3 4 5

QUILT SIZE: 79" x 90³/₄" (200 cm x 231 cm)

FINISHED BLOCK SIZE: 8¹/₄" x 8¹/₄" (21 cm x 21 cm)

PIECED BLOCKS: 42

Yardage Requirements

Yardage is based on 45"w fabric.

- ¹/₈ yd (11 cm) **each** of 21 floral prints
- 2⁷/₈ yds (2.6 m) of cream solid
- ⁷/₈ yd (80 cm) **total** of assorted gold prints
- 3¹/₄ yds (2.9 m) of green floral
- 2¹/₂ yds (2.3 m) of green print for borders
- 5¹/₂ yds (5 m) of backing fabric
- ⁷/₈ yd (80 cm) of binding fabric
- 98" x 86" (218 cm x 101 cm) rectangle of batting

Cutting Out the Pieces

*Follow **Rotary Cutting**, page 133, to cut fabric. All strips are cut across the width of the fabric unless otherwise noted. All measurements include a ¹/₄" seam allowance.*

From each floral print:

- Cut 8 **squares** 2¹/₄" x 2¹/₄" (**A**).
- Cut 2 **squares** 3⁵/₈" x 3⁵/₈". Cut each **square** in half once diagonally to make 4 **triangles** (**B**).
- Cut 2 **squares** 3¹/₄" x 3¹/₄" (**C**).
- Cut 2 **squares** 1⁷/₈" x 1⁷/₈" (**D**).

From cream solid:
- Cut 12 **strips** $2^1/4$"w. From these **strips**, cut 210 **squares** $2^1/4$" x $2^1/4$" (**A**). Cut 42 **squares** in half once diagonally to make 84 **triangles** (**E**).
- Cut 6 **strips** 5"w. From these **strips**, cut 42 **squares** 5" x 5". Cut each **square** in half once diagonally to make 84 **triangles** (**F**).
- Cut 9 **strips** 4"w. From these **strips**, cut 84 **squares** 4" x 4" (**G**).

From assorted gold prints:
- Cut 42 **squares** $4^5/8$" x $4^5/8$" (**H**).

From green floral:
- Cut 8 **strips** $8^3/4$"w. From these **strips**, cut 30 **setting squares** $8^3/4$" x $8^3/4$".
- Cut 1 **strip** $6^3/4$"w. From this **strip**, cut 2 **squares** $6^3/4$" x $6^3/4$". Cut each **square** in half once diagonally to make 4 **corner triangles**.
- Cut 2 **strips** 13"w. From these **strips**, cut 6 **squares** 13" x 13". Cut each **square** in half twice diagonally to make 24 **setting triangles** (you will use 22).
- Cut 1 **strip** $4^1/2$"w. From this **strip**, cut 4 **border squares** $4^1/2$" x $4^1/2$".

From green print for borders:
- Cut 2 **top** and **bottom borders** $4^1/2$" x $74^1/2$".
- Cut 2 **side borders** $4^1/2$" x $86^1/4$".

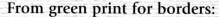

Assembling the Quilt Top

*Follow **Piecing and Pressing**, page 135, to assemble the quilt top. For each block, you will need 8 Triangle-Squares, 2 B's, 1 C, and 1 D from the same print fabric. From cream fabric you will need 2 E's, 2 F's, and 2 G's. From gold fabric you will need 1 H.*

1. Follow **Steps 1-10** of **English Ivy Quilt**, page 86, to make **English Ivy Blocks**.
2. Referring to **Assembly Diagram**, page 93, sew **corner triangles**, **side triangles**, **squares**, and **English Ivy Blocks** into diagonal **Rows**. Sew **Rows** together to make center section of quilt top.
3. Refer to **Steps 13** and **14** of **English Ivy Quilt**, page 88, to sew borders to **Quilt Top**.

Completing the Quilt

1. Follow **Quilting**, page 138, to mark, layer, and quilt as desired. Our quilt is machine quilted in the ditch around the pieced blocks. There are flowers and stems quilted in the setting squares and a scalloped feather quilted in the borders.
2. Cut a 31" square of binding fabric. Follow **Binding**, page 141, to bind quilt using $2^1/2$"w bias binding with mitered corners.

Assembly Diagram

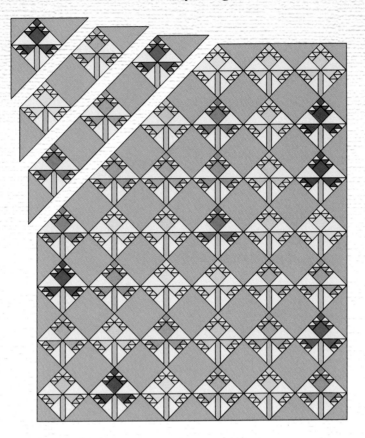

Quilt Top Diagram

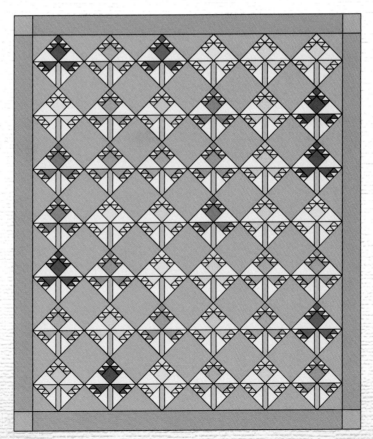

Friendship Album Variation

WHAT CONSTITUTES **A TRUE ALBUM BLOCK** is a matter that could be debated. Most sources tell us that Album Quilts were originally CREATED FOR FUTURE BRIDES BY THEIR FRIENDS, and the major components of any Album Quilt are blocks with LIGHT-COLORED CENTERS expressly for the INSCRIPTION OF SIGNATURES. These "memory" quilts were highly prized keepsakes, especially when a marriage involved the bride relocating to another region of the country and leaving behind friends and family. This circa 1890 album quilt is in near-excellent condition, but was never signed. It has some wear around the edges and a few stains on the reverse, however the fabric still has its original glaze and there are no puckers at seams and along the quilting. This indicates that the quilt has never been washed — a remarkable thing for patchwork that has PASSED THE CENTURY MARK.

STANLEY HOME PRODUCTS, INC.
WESTFIELD, MASS.

40 YDS. OF 4 POPULAR SHADES

FOR MENDING & DARNING

1 END OF 2 PLY

HOUSEHOLD BRUSHES & CHEMICALS
Made in U. S. A.

Friendship Album Variation

SKILL LEVEL: 1 2 3 4 5

QUILT SIZE: 73½" x 90½" (187 cm x 230 cm)

FINISHED BLOCK SIZE: 12½" x 12½" (32 cm x 32 cm)

PIECED BLOCKS: 20

Yardage Requirements

Yardage is based on 45"w fabric.

  $2^5/8$ yds (2.4 m) of red print
  $5/8$ yd (57 cm) of blue print
  $1/8$ yd (11 cm) **each** of 20 light prints
  $1/8$ yd (11 cm) **each** of 20 dark prints
  $5^1/2$ yds (5 m) of backing fabric
  $7/8$ yd (80 cm) of binding fabric
  82" x 98" (208 cm x 249 cm) rectangle
   of batting

Cutting Out the Pieces

Note: *The outer sashing strips on this **Antique Friendship Album Quilt** are not symmetrical, with one side measuring only 2"wide. Our instructions have been written to make the outer sashing strips symmetrical, with the option to duplicate the original quilt.*

*Follow **Rotary Cutting**, page 133, to cut fabric. All strips are cut across the width of the fabric unless otherwise noted. All measurements include a $1/4$" seam allowance.*

From red print:
- Cut 16 **strips** 5"w. From these **strips**, cut 49 **sashing strips** 5" x 13".
  Note: To duplicate the antique quilt, cut 44 sashing strips 5" x 13" and 5 sashing strips $2^1/_2$" x 13".

From blue print:
- Cut 4 **strips** 5"w. From these **strips**, cut 30 **sashing squares** 5" x 5".
  Note: To duplicate the antique quilt, cut 24 sashing squares 5" x 5" and 6 sashing rectangles $2^1/_2$" x 5".

From each light print:
- Cut 1 **strip** 3"w. From this **strip**, cut 10 **squares** 3" x 3".
- Cut 1 **rectangle** 3" x 8".

From each dark print:
- Cut 1 **strip** 3"w. From this **strip**, cut 12 **squares** 3" x 3".

Assembling the Quilt Top

Follow **Piecing and Pressing**, *page 135*, to assemble the quilt top.

1. Referring to **Block Diagram**, sew 1 light **rectangle**, 10 light, and 12 dark **squares** together to make **Block**. Make 20 **Blocks**.

Block
(make 20)

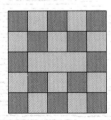

2. Referring to **Row Diagram**, sew 4 **Blocks** and 5 **sashing strips** together to make **Row**. Make 5 **Rows**.
   Note: To duplicate the antique quilt, replace the sashing strip at 1 end of each row with a $2^1/_2$" x 13" sashing strip.

Row
(make 5)

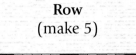

3. Referring to **Sashing Row Diagram**, sew 5 **sashing squares** and 4 **sashing strips** together to make **Sashing Row**. Make 6 **Sashing Rows**.
   Note: To duplicate the antique quilt, replace the sashing square at 1 end of Sashing Row with a $2^1/_2$" x 5" sashing rectangle.

Sashing Row
(make 6)

4. Referring to **Quilt Top Diagram**, page 99, sew **Rows** and **Sashing Rows** together to complete **Quilt Top**.

Completing the Quilt Top

1. Follow **Quilting**, page 138, to mark, layer, and quilt as desired. Our quilt is hand quilted with outline quilting in the blocks, parallel lines in the sashings and an "X" in the sashing squares.
2. Cut a 30" square of binding fabric. Follow **Binding**, page 141, to bind quilt using $2^1/_2$"w bias binding with mitered corners.

BLUE SASHING AND A MIX OF PRINTS IN SUMMERTIME SHADES

MAKE THIS NEW LAP QUILT A PERFECT GIFT FOR A MODERN JUNE BRIDE. Another idea is to choose fabrics in school colors and host a quilting bee for a college-bound student. This quilt is just the right size to fit most dormitory beds.

Friendship Album Variation

SKILL LEVEL: 1 2 3 4 5

QUILT SIZE: 73½" x 90½" (187 cm x 230 cm)

FINISHED BLOCK SIZE: 12½" x 12½" (32 cm x 32 cm)

PIECED BLOCKS: 20

CONTEMPORARY

Yardage Requirements

Yardage is based on 45"w fabric.

2⅝ yds (2.4 m) of blue print
⅝ yd (57 cm) of blue check
⅛ yd (11 cm) **each** of 20 light prints
⅛ yd (11 cm) **each** of 20 dark prints
5½ yds (5 m) of backing fabric
⅞ yd (80 cm) of binding fabric
82" x 98" (208 cm x 249 cm) rectangle
  of batting

Cutting Out the Pieces

*Follow **Rotary Cutting**, page 133, to cut fabric. All strips are cut across the width of the fabric unless otherwise noted. All measurements include a ¼" seam allowance.*

From blue print:
- Cut 16 **strips** 5"w. From these **strips**, cut 49 **sashing strips** 5" x 13".

From blue check:
- Cut 4 **strips** 5"w. From these **strips**, cut 30 **sashing squares** 5" x 5".

From each light print:
- Cut 1 **strip** 3"w. From this **strip** cut 10 **squares** 3" x 3".
- Cut 1 **rectangle** 3" x 8".

From each dark print:
- Cut 1 **strip** 3"w. From this **strip** cut 12 **squares** 3" x 3".

Assembling the Quilt Top

*Follow **Friendship Album Variation** instructions, page 97, to piece **Quilt Top** using blue print for sashing strips and blue check for sashing squares.*

Completing the Quilt Top

1. Follow **Quilting,** page 138, to mark, layer, and quilt as desired. Our quilt is machine quilted with a flower in the blocks, an "X" in the sashing squares, and parallel lines in the sashings.
2. Cut a 30" square of binding fabric. Follow **Binding,** page 141, to bind quilt using $2^1/2$"w bias binding with mitered corners.

Quilt Top Diagram

Double Nine Patch

A QUILT MADE OF NOTHING BUT SQUARES —

GREAT FOR A QUICK FINISH, which may be exactly what the creator

of the DEPRESSION-ERA Double Nine Patch quilt had in mind. Nine

Patch blocks were often STITCHED BY YOUNG GIRLS as they learned

how to use a needle and thread. And if a full-size quilt still seemed

daunting, then a good way for a child to start her

sewing experience was by making doll quilts

from miniature Nine Patch blocks.

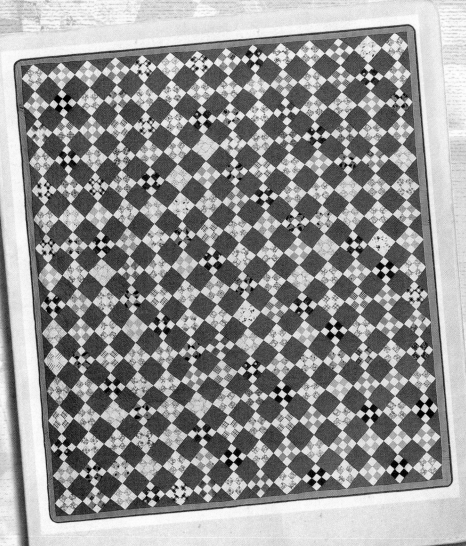

Double Nine Patch

SKILL LEVEL: 1 2 3 4 5

QUILT SIZE: 62½" x 71" (159 cm x 180 cm)

FINISHED BLOCK SIZE: 3" x 3" (8 cm x 8 cm)

PIECED BLOCKS: 224

· CLASSIC ·

Yardage Requirements

Yardage is based on 45"w fabric.
- 2$\frac{1}{4}$ yds (2.1 m) of red solid
- 1$\frac{7}{8}$ yds (1.7 m) of white solid
- $\frac{1}{8}$ yd (11 cm) **each** of 16 assorted prints
- $\frac{1}{2}$ yd (46 cm) of green solid
- 4$\frac{1}{2}$ yds (4.1 m) of backing fabric
- $\frac{7}{8}$ yd (80 cm) of binding fabric
- 71" x 79" (180 cm x 201 cm) rectangle of batting

Cutting out the Pieces

*Follow **Rotary Cutting**, page 133, to cut fabric. All strips are cut across the width of the fabric unless otherwise noted. All measurements include a $\frac{1}{4}$" seam allowance.*

From red solid:
- Cut 17 **strips** 3$\frac{1}{2}$"w. From these **strips**, cut 195 **setting squares** 3$\frac{1}{2}$" x 3$\frac{1}{2}$".
- Cut 2 squares 3" x 3". Cut **squares** in half once diagonally to make 4 **corner triangles**.
- Cut 2 strips 5$\frac{1}{2}$"w. From these strips, cut 14 squares 5$\frac{1}{2}$" x 5$\frac{1}{2}$". Cut **squares** in half twice diagonally to make 56 **setting triangles**.

From white solid:
- Cut 40 **strips** 1$\frac{1}{2}$"w. Cut 8 **strips** in half to make 16 **strips** 1$\frac{1}{2}$" x 21".

From each assorted print:
- Cut 1 **strip** 1$\frac{1}{2}$"w.
- Cut 2 **strips** 1$\frac{1}{2}$ x 21".

From green solid:
- Cut 2 **top** and **bottom borders** 1$\frac{1}{2}$" x 64", piecing as necessary.
- Cut 2 **side borders** 1$\frac{1}{2}$" x 74$\frac{1}{2}$", piecing as necessary.

Assembling the Quilt Top

*Follow **Piecing and Pressing**, page 135, to assemble the quilt top.*

1. Refer to **Strip Set Diagrams** to sew 1 print and 2 white 1$\frac{1}{2}$" x 42" **strips** together to make **Strip Set A**. Sew 2 print and 1 white 1$\frac{1}{2}$" x 21" **strips** together to make **Strip Set B**. Cut across each **Strip Set** at 1$\frac{1}{2}$" intervals to make a total of 28 **Unit 1's** and 14 **Unit 2's**.

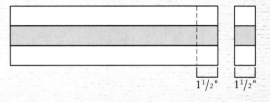

Strip Set A   Unit 1 (cut 28)

1$\frac{1}{2}$"   1$\frac{1}{2}$"

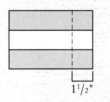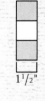

Strip Set B   Unit 2 (cut 14)

1$\frac{1}{2}$"   1$\frac{1}{2}$"

2. Assemble 2 **Unit 1's** and 1 **Unit 2** as shown to make **Nine-Patch Block**. Make 14 **Nine-Patch Blocks**.

Nine-Patch Block
(make 14)

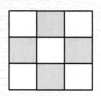

3. Repeat **Steps 1** and **2** with remaining **strips** to make a total of 224 **Nine-Patch Blocks**.
4. Referring to **Assembly Diagram**, sew **corner triangles**, **setting triangles**, **setting squares**, and **Nine-Patch Blocks** into diagonal **Rows**. Sew **Rows** together to make center section of quilt top.
5. Referring to **Adding Squared Borders**, page 137, sew **top** and **bottom borders**, then **side borders** to center section to complete **Quilt Top**.

Completing the Quilt

1. Follow **Quilting**, page 138, to mark, layer and quilt as desired. Our quilt is hand quilted with diagonal lines over the entire quilt top.
2. Referring to photo, page 106, trim corners of **Quilt Top** to round edges.
3. Cut a 28" square of binding fabric. Follow **Making Continuous Bias Strip Binding**, page 141, to make $2^1/2$"w bias binding. Follow **Steps 1** and **2** of **Attaching Binding with Mitered Corners** to pin binding to front of quilt, easing binding around curved edges. Sew binding to quilt until binding overlaps beginning end by approximately 2". Trim excess binding. Trim backing and batting a scant $^1/4$" larger than quilt top to fill the binding when it is folded over to the quilt backing. Fold binding over to quilt backing and pin in place, covering stitching line. Blindstitch binding to backing.

I CANNOT COUNT **MY DAY** *complete* 'TIL **NEEDLE, THREAD,** AND **FABRIC** MEET.

∽ **Unknown**

❖

THERE'S NEVER A *new* FASHION BUT IT'S *old.*

∽ **Chaucer,** *The Canterbury Tales*

TODAY'S ENORMOUS SELECTION OF FABRIC COLORS ENCOURAGES
ALL QUILTERS TO REDISCOVER THE JOY OF CONSTRUCTING QUILT TOPS FROM SIMPLE SQUARES.

The use of color on our modern rendition rounds the corners and softens the angles. The small-to-medium prints also create

a gentle grading of hues from one block to the next, giving the quilt "movement" that the eye can more easily follow.

Double Nine Patch

SKILL LEVEL: 1 2 3 4 5

QUILT SIZE: 41" x 58" (104 cm x 147 cm)

FINISHED BLOCK SIZE: 3" x 3" (8 cm x 8 cm)

PIECED BLOCKS: 96

Yardage Requirements

Yardage is based on 45"w fabric.

$^3/_4$ yd (69 cm) of wine floral print
$^1/_4$ yd (23 cm) of green floral print
$^1/_4$ yd (23 cm) of gold floral print
$2^1/_4$ yds (2.1 m) of white solid
2 rectangles 2" x 18" (5 cm x 46 cm) of
  16 assorted pink prints
1 rectangle 2" x 18" (5 cm x 46 cm) of
  10 assorted green prints
1 rectangle 2" x 18" (5 cm x 46 cm) of
  6 assorted gold prints
$1^5/_8$ yds (1.5 m) of green print for borders
$3^3/_4$ yds (3.4 m) of backing fabric
$^3/_4$ yd (69 cm) of binding fabric
49" x 66" (124 cm x 168 cm) rectangle
  of batting

Cutting out the Pieces

*Follow **Rotary Cutting**, page 133, to cut fabric. All strips are cut across the width of the fabric unless otherwise noted. All measurements include a $^1/_4$" seam allowance.*

From wine floral print:
- Cut 3 **strips** $3^1/_2$"w. From these **strips**, cut 32 **setting squares** $3^1/_2$" x $3^1/_2$".
- Cut 2 **squares** 3 x 3". Cut **squares** in half once diagonally to make 4 **corner triangles**.
- Cut 2 **strips** $5^1/_2$"w. From these **strips**, cut 9 **squares** $5^1/_2$" x $5^1/_2$". Cut **squares** in half twice diagonally to make 36 **setting triangles**.

From green floral print:
- Cut 2 **strips** $3^1/_2$"w. From these **strips**, cut 24 **setting squares** $3^1/_2$" x $3^1/_2$".

From gold floral print:
- Cut 2 **strips** 3¹/₂"w. From these **strips**, cut 21 **setting squares** 3¹/₂" x 3¹/₂".

From green print for borders:
- Cut 2 **top** and **bottom borders** 3¹/₂" x 44¹/₂".
- Cut 2 **side borders** 3¹/₂" x 55¹/₂".

From white solid:
- Cut 48 **strips** 1¹/₂" x 32". Cut each **strip** in half twice to make 192 **strips** 8" long. Cut 48 of the 8" **strips** in half to make 96 **strips** 4" long.

From each pink print:
- Cut 1 **strip** 1¹/₂" x 16". Cut **strip** into one 8" and two 4" lengths.

From each green print:
- Cut 1 **strip** 1¹/₂" x 16". Cut **strip** into one 8" and two 4" lengths.

From each gold print:
- Cut 1 **strip** 1¹/₂" x 16". Cut **strip** into one 8" and two 4" lengths.

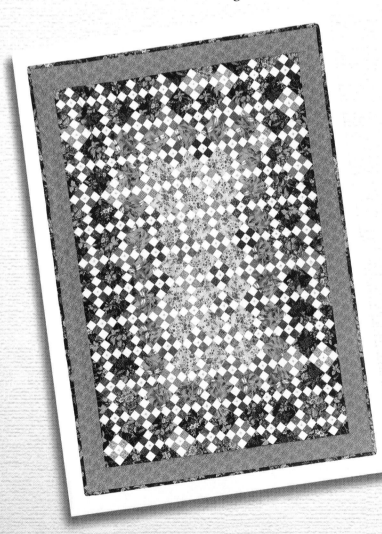

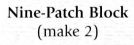

Follow **Piecing and Pressing**, page 135, to assemble the quilt top. You will make 4 Nine-Patch Blocks from each pink print and 2 from each green and gold print.

1. Referring to **Strip Set Diagrams**, sew 1 print and 2 white 1¹/₂" x 8" **strips** together to make **Strip Set A**. Sew 1 white and 2 print 1¹/₂" x 4" **strips** together to make **Strip Set B**. Cut across each **Strip Set** at 1¹/₂" intervals to make a total of 4 **Unit 1's** and 2 **Unit 2's**.

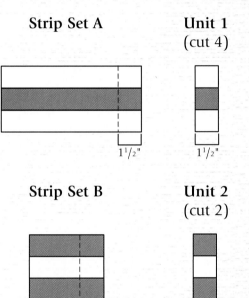

2. Assemble 2 **Unit 1's** and 1 **Unit 2** as shown to make **Nine-Patch Block**. Make 2 **Nine-Patch Blocks**.

Nine-Patch Block
(make 2)

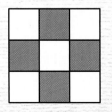

3. Repeat **Steps 1** and **2** with remaining **strips** to make a total of 96 **Nine-Patch Blocks**.
4. Referring to **Assembly Diagram**, sew **corner triangles**, **side triangles**, **squares**, and **Nine-Patch Blocks** into diagonal **Rows**. Sew **Rows** together to make center section of quilt top.
5. Referring to **Quilt Top Diagram** and following **Adding Squared Borders**, page 137, sew **side**, then **top** and **bottom borders** to center section to complete **Quilt Top**.

Assembly Diagram

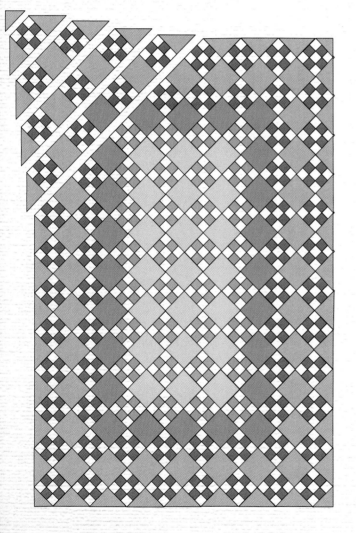

Completing the Quilt

1. Follow **Quilting,** page 138, to mark, layer and quilt as desired. Our quilt is machine quilted with flowers in the Nine-Patch Blocks and a leaf pattern in the setting squares and borders.
2. Cut a 24" square of binding fabric. Follow **Binding,** page 141, to bind quilt using $2^{1}/_{2}$"w bias binding with mitered corners.

Quilt Top Diagram

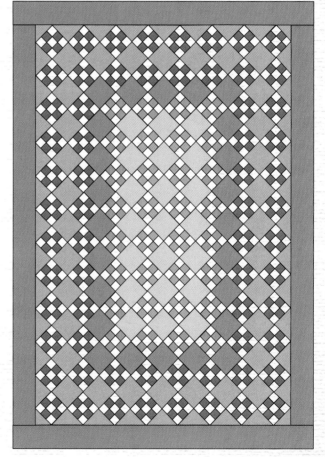

Strippy Diamond Squares

YOU CAN ALMOST SEE THE CREATOR OF THIS **UNFINISHED QUILT TOP**

sorting through her scrap bag, trying to decide how to make something attractive

from a sack of mostly drab fabrics. The pattern she chose, with its HODGE-PODGE

OF STRIPPY PIECES forming bright red diamonds, seems to indicate that she had

only irregular scraps and very little time with which to work. The FRAGMENTS OF

NEWSPRINT IN THE SEAMS show us that she used foundation piecing for her

blocks. On one or two shreds of newspaper, the date "Friday, April 1" and the

words "Springfield, Missouri" can be found. And the phrase "they arrived in an

automobile" leads us to speculate that the "April 1" in reference occurred in either

1910 or 1921. During that period of time, automobiles were uncommon sights in

the Ozark Mountain region and would have generated a good deal of interest.

Strippy Diamond Squares

SKILL LEVEL: 1 2 3 4 5

QUILT SIZE: 65" X 81" (165 cm x 206 cm)

FINISHED BLOCK SIZE: 8" x 8" (20 cm x 20 cm)

PIECED BLOCKS: 80

· CLASSIC ·

Yardage Requirements

Yardage is based on 45"w fabric.

$5^1/_2$ yds (5 m) **total** of assorted black, gray, blue, and neutral prints

$1^7/_8$ yds (1.7 m) of red print

5 yds (4.6 m) of backing fabric

$^7/_8$ yd (80 cm) of binding fabric

73" x 89" (185 cm x 226 cm) rectangle of batting

You will also need:

Paper or tear-away stabilizer for foundations

Square ruler 9" x 9" (23 cm x 23 cm) or larger

Cutting Out the Pieces

*Follow **Rotary Cutting**, page 133, to cut fabric. All measurements include a $^1/_4$" seam allowance.*

From red print:

- Cut 27 **strips** 2"w. From these **strips**, cut 80 **center strips** 2" x $12^1/_2$".

From assorted black, gray, blue, and neutral prints:

- Cutting lengths and widths for **strips** will vary. The longest **strip** used is $12^1/_2$" and the widest **strip** is 5". Number of **strips** used will vary with widths used. Some **strips** are cut wedge-shaped and some only use 1 **strip** per side in addition to the **center strip**.

Assembling the Quilt Top

*Follow **Piecing and Pressing**, page 135, to assemble the quilt top. Use a $^1/_4$" seam allowance for all sewing.*

1. You will need to make 80 paper or stabilizer squares. If using paper, you can either draw each square or draw 1 square then make photocopies. If using stabilizer, you will have to draw each square.

2. On paper or stabilizer, draw a square $9^1/_2$" x $9^1/_2$". Cut out square along drawn lines. Referring to **Fig. 1**, draw a diagonal line (**Line 1**) across the center of the foundation square. Draw **Line 2** $^1/_4$" away from **Line 1**.

Fig. 1

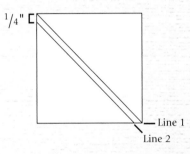

3. With right side of **center strip** up, place 1 raw edge on **Line 2**. Pin or baste **center strip** in place (**Fig. 2**).

   Fig. 2

4. Cut 1 **strip** of print fabric 10" long by desired width and shape (**strip 2**). With right sides together and raw edges matching, lay **strip 2** on top of **center strip**. Using a $^1/_4$" seam allowance and a small stitch length, sew **strip 2** and **center strip** to foundation square (**Fig. 3**). Fold **strip 2** back to expose right side and press (**Fig. 4**).

   Fig. 3

   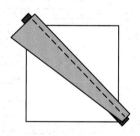

   Fig. 4

5. Repeat **Step 4** to continue adding **strips**, decreasing length of each **strip** as you work toward each corner, until foundation square is completely covered (**Fig. 5**).

   Fig. 5

   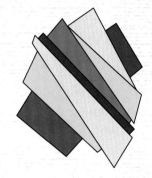

6. Referring to **Fig. 6** and keeping bottom edge of **center strip** straight on diagonal line of ruler, square up **Block** to $8^1/_2$". Repeat **Steps 2-6** to make 80 **Blocks**.

   Fig. 6

   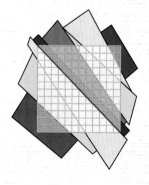

   Block
   (make 80)

7. Referring to **Row Diagrams**, sew 8 **Blocks** together to make **Row**. Make 10 **Rows**. Remove paper or stabilizer from seam allowances.

Row
(make 10)

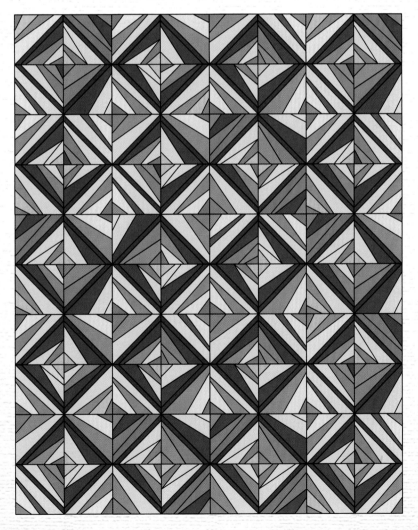

8. Referring to **Quilt Top Diagram**, sew **Rows** together to complete center section of **Quilt Top**. Remove remaining paper or stabilizer foundations.

1. Follow **Quilting,** page 138, to mark, layer, and quilt as desired. Our **Quilt Top** was never quilted.
2. Cut a 29" square of binding fabric. Follow **Binding,** page 141, to bind quilt using $2^1/_2$"w bias binding with mitered corners.

Quilt Top Diagram

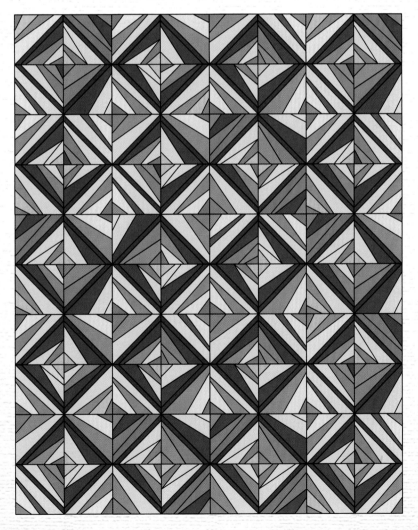

OUR MODERN VERSION OF STRIPPY DIAMOND SQUARES USES CHEERY CONVERSATION PRINTS AND FLORAL FABRICS IN THE HAPPY SHADES OF SPRINGTIME. Re-create this happy lap quilt in your own choice of colors. Quick-piecing may inspire you to keep making the zippy blocks until your quilt is large enough to warm a bed.

Strippy Diamond Squares

SKILL LEVEL: 1 2 3 4 5

QUILT SIZE: 58" X 58" (147 cm x 147 cm)

FINISHED BLOCK SIZE: 8" x 8" (20 cm x 20 cm)

PIECED BLOCKS: 36

Yardage Requirements

Yardage is based on 45"w fabric.

- $3^1/_2$ yds (3.2 m) **total** of assorted light and medium prints
- $1^5/_8$ yds (1.5 m) of green print
- $1^7/_8$ yds (1.7 cm) yellow floral stripe
- $3^5/_8$ yds (3.3 m) of backing fabric
- $^3/_4$ yd (69 cm) of binding fabric
- 66" x 66" (168 cm x 168 cm) rectangle of batting

You will also need:

- Paper or tear-away stabilizer for foundations
- Square ruler 9" x 9" (22.9 cm x 22.9 cm) or larger

Cutting Out the Pieces

Follow **Rotary Cutting**, *page 133, to cut fabric. Cut* **borders** *along the length of the fabric before cutting* **strips**. *Cut* **strips** *across the remaining width of the fabric. All measurements include a* $^1/_4$" *seam allowance.*

From green print:

- Cut 2 **top** and **bottom inner borders** $1^1/_2$" x $52^1/_2$".
- Cut 2 **side inner borders** $1^1/_2$" x $54^1/_2$".
- From remaining width, cut 18 **strips** 2"w. From these strips, cut 36 **center strips** 2" x $12^1/_2$".

From yellow floral stripe:
- Cut 2 **top** and **bottom outer borders** 4" x 54$\frac{1}{2}$".
- Cut 2 **side outer borders** 4" x 61$\frac{1}{2}$".

From assorted light and medium prints:
- Cutting lengths and widths for **strips** will vary. The longest **strip** used is 12$\frac{1}{2}$" and the widest **strip** is 5". Number of **strips** used will vary with widths used. Some **strips** are cut wedge-shaped and others are fussy cut to showcase a motif.

Assembling the Quilt Top

*Follow **Piecing and Pressing**, page 135, to assemble the quilt top.*

1. You will need to make 36 paper or stabilizer squares. If using paper, you can either draw each square or draw 1 square then make photocopies. If using stabilizer, you will have to draw each square.
2. Follow **Steps 2-6** of **Strippy Diamond Squares Quilt**, page 117, to make 36 **Blocks**.

3. Follow **Steps 7** and **8**, page 119, and refer to **Quilt Top Diagram** to sew 6 **Blocks** together to make a **Row**. Make 6 **Rows**. Sew **Rows** together to make center section of quilt top.

4. Follow **Adding Squared Borders**, page 137, to sew **top** and **bottom inner borders**, then **side inner borders** to center section. Repeat to add **outer borders** to center section to complete piecing the **Quilt Top**.

1. Follow **Quilting,** page 138, to mark, layer, and quilt as desired. Our quilt is machine quilted with geometric patterns in the blocks and borders.

2. Cut a 26" square of binding fabric. Follow **Binding**, page 141, to bind quilt using $2^{1}/_{2}$"w bias binding with mitered corners.

Quilt Top Diagram

Rail Fence Variation

THIS AMAZING QUILT IS OSTENSIBLY **FROM THE 1880'S,**
but shows absolutely no wear. Its colors are true with no fading (not
even the purples!) and the fabrics have retained their glaze. Also,
many of these FABRICS HAVE BEEN REPRODUCED in recent years,
which tempts one to think this particular quilt is younger than its
apparent style. Either way, the quilt is a beauty that SHOULD BE
TREASURED for many more years to come.

Rail Fence Variation

SKILL LEVEL: 1 2 3 4 5

QUILT SIZE: 76¼ x 76¼ (194 cm x 194 cm)

FINISHED BLOCK SIZE: 8¾" x 8¾" (22 cm x 22 cm)

PIECED BLOCKS: 49

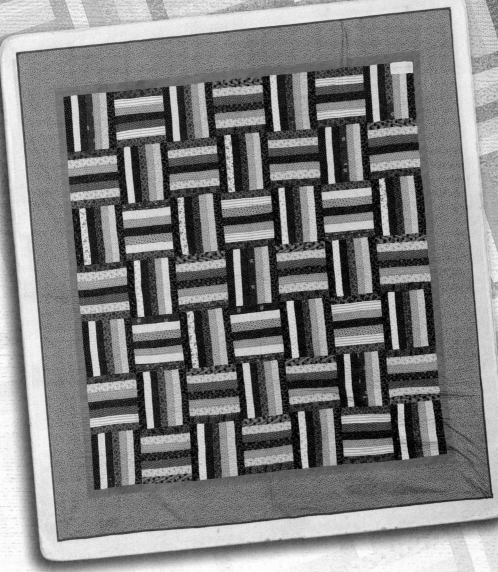

Yardage Requirements

Yardage is based on 45"w fabric.

$1\frac{1}{2}$ yds (1.4 cm) **total** of assorted
dark prints

$1\frac{1}{2}$ yds (1.4 cm) **total** of assorted
light prints

2 yds (1.8 m) **total** of assorted
medium prints

2 yds (1.8 m) of blue solid

$2\frac{1}{4}$ yds (2.1 m) of pink print

$4\frac{3}{4}$ yds (4.3 m) of backing fabric

$\frac{7}{8}$ yd (80 cm) of binding fabric

85" x 85" (216 cm x 216 cm) square
of batting

Cutting Out the Pieces

Follow **Rotary Cutting**, page 133, to cut fabric.
All measurements include a $\frac{1}{4}$" seam
allowance. Borders are cut along the lengthwise
grain of the fabric.

From assorted dark prints:
- Cut 26 **strips** $1\frac{3}{4}$"w.

From assorted light prints:
- Cut 26 **strips** $1\frac{3}{4}$"w.

From assorted medium prints:
- Cut 39 **strips** $1\frac{3}{4}$"w.

From blue solid:
- Cut 2 **top** and **bottom inner borders** $1^3/_4$" x $65^3/_4$".
- Cut 2 **side inner borders** $1^3/_4$" x $69^1/_4$".

From pink print:
- Cut 2 **top** and **bottom outer borders** $6^1/_4$" x $69^1/_4$".
- Cut 2 **side outer borders** $6^1/_4$" x $79^3/_4$".

Assembling the Quilt Top

*Follow **Piecing and Pressing**, page 135, to assemble the quilt top.*

1. Referring to **Strip Set Diagram**, sew 2 **dark**, 2 **light**, and 3 **medium strips** together to make 1 **Strip Set**. Make 13 **Strip Sets**.

Strip Set
(make 13)

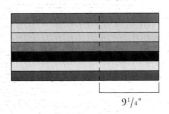

$9^1/_4$"

2. Cut across **Strip Sets** at $9^1/_4$" intervals to make **Rail Fence Block**. Make 49 **Rail Fence Blocks**.

Rail Fence Block
(Make 49)

3. Referring to **Quilt Top Diagram** for orientation, sew 7 **Rail Fence Blocks** together to make **Row**. Make 7 **Rows**.
4. Follow **Adding Squared Borders**, page 137, to sew **top** and **bottom inner borders**, then **side borders** to center section. Repeat to add **outer borders** to center section to complete piecing the **Quilt Top**.

Completing the Quilt Top

1. Follow **Quilting**, page 138, to mark, layer and quilt as desired. Our quilt is hand quilted with alternating parallel diagonal or horizontal straight lines in each block. The borders are quilted with parallel diagonal lines.
2. Cut a 30" square of binding fabric. Follow **Binding**, page 141, to bind quilt using $2^1/_2$"w bias binding with mitered corners.

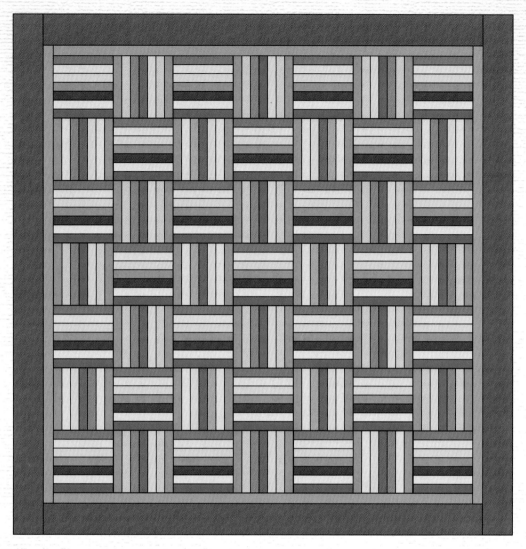

 IT IS NOT THAT **ARTISTIC POWER** HAS LEFT THE WORLD,

BUT THAT A MORE **RAPID LIFE** HAS DEVELOPED ITSELF IN IT, LEAVING NO TIME

FOR DELIBERATE *dainty decoration* OR **LABOURS OF LOVE**.

— Mrs. Orrinsmith, 1877

THE RAIL FENCE PATTERN IS QUICK TO STITCH, ESPECIALLY WITH ROTARY CUTTING AND PIECING

TECHNIQUES. It's a great way to showcase both vintage and reproduction fabrics. Use a hodge-podge of your fabric

scraps to get the classic utility quilt look, or match your colors carefully to create a masterpiece of shading.

Rail Fence Variation

SKILL LEVEL: 1 2 3 4 5

QUILT SIZE: 27" x 27" (69 cm x 69 cm)

FINISHED BLOCK SIZE: $8^3/_4$" x $8^3/_4$" (22 cm x 22 cm)

PIECED BLOCKS: 4

Yardage Requirements

Yardage is based on 45"w fabric.

$^3/_8$ yd (34 cm) **total** of assorted bright prints

$^1/_4$ yd (23 cm) of green print

$^1/_2$ yd (46 cm) of yellow print

$^7/_8$ yd (80 cm) of backing fabric

$^1/_2$ yd (46 cm) of binding fabric

35" x 35" (89 cm x 89 cm) square of batting

Cutting Out the Pieces

Follow **Rotary Cutting**, page 133, to cut fabric. All measurements include a $^1/_4$" seam allowance.

From assorted bright prints:
- Cut 28 **rectangles** $1^3/_4$" x $9^1/_4$".

From green print:
- Cut 2 **top** and **bottom inner borders** $1^3/_4$" x 22".
- Cut 2 **side inner borders** $1^3/_4$" x $24^1/_2$".

From yellow print:
- Cut 2 **top** and **bottom outer borders** $3^1/2$" x $24^1/2$".
- Cut 2 **side outer borders** $3^1/2$" x $30^1/2$".

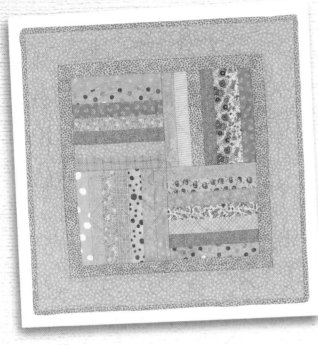

Assembling the Quilt Top

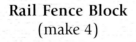

*Follow **Piecing and Pressing**, page 135, to assemble the quilt top.*

1. Referring to **Block Diagram**, sew 7 **rectangles** together to make **Rail Fence Block**. Make 4 **Rail Fence Blocks**.

Rail Fence Block
(make 4)

2. Referring to **Quilt Top Diagram**, sew 4 **Blocks** together to make center section of quilt top.
3. Follow **Adding Squared Borders**, page 137, to sew **top** and **bottom inner borders**, then **side inner borders** to center section. Repeat to add **outer borders** to center section to complete piecing the **Quilt Top**.

Completing the Quilt Top

1. Follow **Quilting**, page 138, to mark, layer and quilt as desired. Our quilt is machine quilted with flowers in the outer border and concentric circles and squares in the blocks.
2. Cut a 16" square of binding fabric. Follow **Binding**, page 141, to bind quilt using $2^1/2$"w bias binding with mitered corners.

Quilt Top Diagram

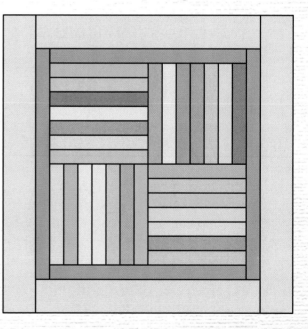

General INSTRUCTIONS

COMPLETE INSTRUCTIONS ARE GIVEN FOR MAKING EACH OF THE PROJECTS SHOWN IN THIS BOOK. To make your project easier and more enjoyable, we encourage you to carefully read all of the general instructions, study the color photographs, and familiarize yourself with the individual project instructions before beginning a project.

Rotary Cutting

*Based on the idea that you can easily cut strips of fabric and then cut those strips into smaller pieces, rotary cutting has brought speed and accuracy to quiltmaking. Observe safety precautions when using the rotary cutter, since it is extremely sharp. Develop a habit of retracting the blade guard **just before** making a cut and closing it **immediately afterward**, before laying down the cutter.*

1. Wash, dry, and press fabrics.
2. Cut all strips from the selvage-to-selvage width of the fabric unless otherwise indicated in project instructions. Place fabric on the cutting mat, as shown in **Fig. 1**, with the fold of the fabric toward you. To straighten the uneven fabric edge, make the first "squaring up" cut by placing the right edge of the rotary cutting ruler over the left raw edge of the fabric. Place right-angle triangle (or another rotary cutting ruler) with the lower edge carefully aligned with the fold and the left edge against the ruler (**Fig. 1**). Hold the ruler firmly with your left hand, placing your little finger off the left edge to anchor the ruler. Remove the triangle, pick up the rotary cutter, and retract the blade guard. Using a smooth downward motion, make the cut by running the blade of the rotary cutter firmly along the right edge of the ruler (**Fig. 2**). **Always** cut in a direction away from your body and **immediately** close the blade guard after each cut.

Fig. 1

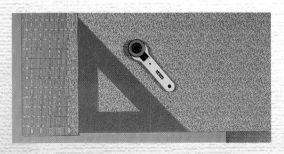

Fig. 2

3. To cut each of the strips required for a project, place the ruler over the cut edge of the fabric, aligning desired marking on the ruler with the cut edge (**Fig. 3**); make the cut. When cutting several strips from a single piece of fabric, it is important to occasionally use the ruler and triangle to ensure that cuts are still at a perfect right angle to the fold. If not, repeat Step 2 to straighten.

Fig. 3

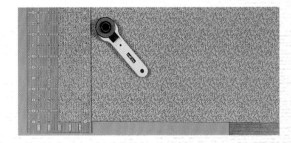

4. To square up selvage ends of a strip before cutting pieces, refer to **Fig. 4** and place folded strip on mat with selvage ends to your right. Aligning a horizontal marking on ruler with 1 long edge of strip, use rotary cutter to trim selvage to make end of strip square and even (**Fig. 4**). Turn strip (or entire mat) so that cut end is to your left before making subsequent cuts.

Fig. 4

5. Pieces such as rectangles and squares can now be cut from strips. Usually strips remain folded, and pieces are cut in pairs after ends of strips are squared up. To cut squares or rectangles from a strip, place ruler over left end of strip, aligning desired marking on ruler with cut end of strip. To ensure perfectly square cuts, align a horizontal marking on ruler with 1 long edge of strip (**Fig. 5**) before making the cut.

Fig. 5

6. To cut 2 triangles from a square, cut square the size indicated in the project instructions. Cut square once diagonally to make 2 triangles (**Fig. 6**).

Fig. 6

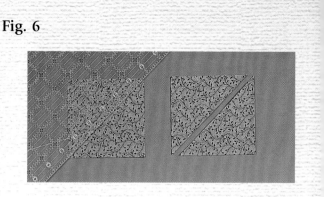

7. To cut 4 triangles from a square, cut square the size indicated in the project instructions. Cut square twice diagonally to make 4 triangles (**Fig. 7**). You may find it helpful to use a small rotary cutting mat so that the mat can be turned to make second cut without disturbing fabric pieces.

Fig. 7

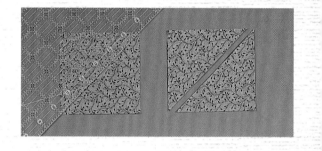

8. After some practice, you may want to try stacking up to 6 fabric layers when making cuts. When stacking strips, match long cut edges and follow Step 4 to square up ends of strip stack. Carefully turn stack (or entire mat) so that squared-up ends are to your left before making subsequent cuts. After cutting, check accuracy of pieces. Some shapes, such as diamonds, are more difficult to cut accurately in stacks.

9. In some cases, strips will be sewn together into strip sets before being cut into smaller units. When cutting a strip set, align a seam in strip set with a horizontal marking on the ruler to maintain square cuts (**Fig. 8**). We do not recommend stacking strip sets for rotary cutting.

Fig. 8

10. Most borders for quilts in this book are cut along the more stable lengthwise grain to minimize wavy edges caused by stretching. To remove selvages before cutting lengthwise strips, place fabric on mat with selvages to your left and squared-up end at bottom of mat. Placing ruler over selvage and using squared-up edge instead of fold, follow Step 2 to cut away selvages as you did raw edges (**Fig. 9**). After making a cut the length of the mat, move the next section of fabric to be cut onto the mat. Repeat until you have removed selvages from required length of fabric.

Fig. 9

11. After removing selvages, place ruler over left edge of fabric, aligning desired marking on ruler with cut edge of fabric. Make cuts as in Step 3. After each cut, move next section of fabric onto mat as in Step 10.

Template Cutting

Our piecing template patterns include a $^1/_4$" seam allowance. Patterns for appliqué templates do not include seam allowances. When cutting instructions say to cut in reverse, place the template upside down on the fabric to cut piece in reverse.

1. To make a template from a pattern, use a permanent fine-point pen to carefully trace the pattern onto template plastic, making sure to transfer all markings. Cut out template along outer drawn line. Check template against original pattern for accuracy.
2. To use a piecing template, place template on wrong side of fabric (unless otherwise indicated), aligning grain line on template with straight grain of fabric. Use a sharp fabric marking pencil to draw around template. Cut out fabric piece using scissors or rotary cutting equipment.
3. To use appliqué templates, place template on right side of fabric. Use a mechanical pencil with a very fine lead to draw around template on fabric. Use scissors to cut out appliqué a scant $^1/_4$" outside drawn line.

Piecing and Pressing

Precise cutting, followed by accurate piecing and careful pressing, will ensure that all the pieces of your quilt top fit together well.

PIECING
Set sewing machine stitch length for approximately 11 stitches per inch. Use a new, sharp needle suited for medium-weight woven fabric.

Use a neutral-colored general-purpose sewing thread (not quilting thread) in the needle and in the bobbin. Stitch first on a scrap of fabric to check upper and bobbin thread tension; make any adjustments necessary.

For good results, it is **essential** that you stitch with an **accurate** $^1/_4$" **seam allowance**. On many sewing machines, the measurement from the needle to the outer edge of the presser foot is $^1/_4$". If this is the case with your machine, the presser foot is your best guide. If not, measure $^1/_4$" from the needle and mark throat plate with a piece of masking tape. Special presser feet that are exactly $^1/_4$" wide are also available for most sewing machines.

When piecing, always place pieces **right sides** together and match raw edges; pin if necessary. (If using straight pins, remove the pins just before they reach the sewing machine needle.)

Sewing Across Seam Intersections

When sewing across the intersection of 2 seams, place pieces right sides together and match seams exactly, making sure seam allowances are pressed in opposite directions (**Fig. 10**). To prevent fabric from shifting, you may wish to pin in place.

Fig. 10

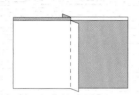

Sewing Strip Sets

When there are several strips to assemble into a strip set, first sew the strips together into pairs, then sew the pairs together to form the strip set. To help avoid distortion, sew 1 seam in 1 direction and then sew the next seam in the opposite direction (**Fig. 11**).

Fig. 11

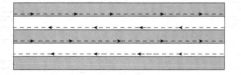

Making Triangle-Squares

The "Stitch and Flip" method is a way to sew bias seams before cutting, making them less likely to stretch during stitching. It uses squares and/or rectangles as specified in the individual project instructions.

With right sides together and lighter color on top, place 2 squares together. Draw a diagonal line across square. Stitch ¹/₄" on each side of drawn line (**Fig. 12**). Use a ruler and rotary cutter to cut apart on drawn line (**Fig. 13**). Repeat to make number of Triangle-Squares needed for project.

Fig. 12   **Fig. 13**

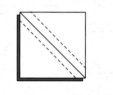

Carefully press Triangle-Squares open, pressing seam allowance toward darker fabric. Trim off points that extend beyond edges of Triangle-Squares (**Fig. 14**).

Fig. 14

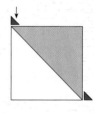

PRESSING

Use a steam iron set on "Cotton" for all pressing. Press as you sew, taking care to prevent small folds along seam lines. Seam allowances are almost always pressed to one side, usually toward the darker fabric. However, to reduce bulk it may occasionally be necessary to press seam allowances toward the lighter fabric or even to press them open. In order to prevent a dark fabric seam allowance from showing through a light fabric, trim the darker seam allowance slightly narrower than the lighter seam allowance. To press long seams, such as those in long strip sets, without curving or other distortion, lay strips across the width of the ironing board.

Appliqué

Needle-Turn Appliqué

In this traditional hand appliqué method, the needle is used to turn the seam allowance under as you sew the appliqué to the background fabric using a Blind Stitch, page 143 (Fig. 41). When stitching, match the color of thread to the color of appliqué to disguise your stitches. Appliqué each piece starting with the ones directly on the background fabric. It is not necessary to appliqué areas that will be covered by another appliqué. Stitches on the right side of fabric should not show. Stitches on the edge of an appliqué and on background fabric should be equal in length. Clipped areas should be secured with a few extra stitches to prevent fraying.

1. Place template on right side of appliqué fabric. Use a pencil to lightly draw around template, leaving at least $1/2$" between shapes; repeat for number of appliqués specified in project instructions.
2. Cut out shapes a scant $1/4$" outside drawn line. Clip inside curves and points up to, but not through, drawn line. Arrange shapes on background fabric and pin or baste in place.
3. Thread a sharps needle with a single strand of general-purpose sewing thread the color of the appliqué; knot one end.
4. Pin center of appliqué to right side of background fabric. Begin on as straight an edge as possible and use point of needle to turn under a small amount of seam allowance, concealing drawn line on appliqué. Blindstitch appliqué to the background, turning under the seam allowance and stitching to completely secure appliqué.

Preparing Fusible Appliqués

Patterns for fused appliqués are printed in reverse to enable you to use our speedy method of preparing appliqués. White or light-colored fabrics may need to be lined with fusible interfacing before applying fusible web to prevent darker fabrics from showing through.

1. Place paper-backed fusible web, web side down, over appliqué pattern. Use a pencil to trace pattern onto paper side of web as many times as indicated in project instructions for a single fabric. Repeat for additional patterns and fabrics.
2. Follow manufacturer's instructions to fuse traced patterns to wrong side of fabrics. Do not remove paper backing.
3. Use scissors to cut out appliqué pieces along traced lines.

Borders

Borders cut along the lengthwise grain will lie flatter than borders cut along the crosswise grain. Cutting lengths given for most borders in this book include an extra 2" of length at each end for "insurance"; borders will be trimmed after measuring completed center section of quilt top.

ADDING SQUARED BORDERS

1. Mark the center of each edge of quilt top.
2. To add side borders, measure across center of quilt top to determine length of borders (**Fig. 15**). Trim side borders to the determined length.

Fig. 15

3. Mark center of 1 long edge of side border. Matching center marks and raw edges, pin border to quilt top, easing in any fullness; stitch. Repeat for other side border.

4. Measure center of quilt top, including attached borders, to determine length of top and bottom borders. Trim top and bottom borders to the determined length. Repeat Step 3 to add borders to quilt top (**Fig. 16**).

Fig. 16

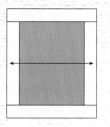

ADDING MITERED BORDERS

1. Mark the center of each edge of quilt top.
2. Mark center of 1 long edge of top border. Measure across center of quilt top (see **Fig. 16**). Matching center marks and raw edges, pin border to center of quilt top edge. Beginning at center of border, measure ¹/₂ the width of the quilt top in both directions and mark. Match marks on border with corners of quilt top and pin. Easing in any fullness, pin border to quilt top. Sew border to quilt top, beginning and ending seam exactly ¹/₄" from each corner of quilt top and backstitching at beginning and end of stitching (**Fig. 17**).

Fig. 17

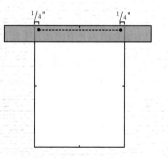

3. Repeat Step 2 to sew bottom, then side borders to quilt top. To keep top and bottom borders out of the way when attaching side borders, fold and pin as shown in **Fig. 18**.

Fig. 18

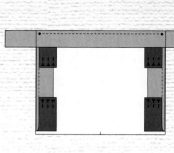

4. Fold 1 corner of quilt top diagonally with right sides together and matching edges. Use ruler to mark stitching line as shown in **Fig. 19**. Pin borders together along drawn line. Sew on drawn line, backstitching at beginning and end of stitching (**Fig. 20**).

Fig. 19   **Fig. 20**

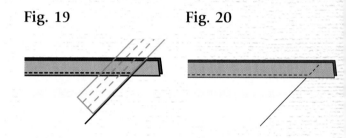

5. Turn mitered corner right side up. Check to make sure corner will lie flat with no gaps or puckers.
6. Trim seam allowance to ¹/₄"; press to one side.
7. Repeat Steps 4-6 to miter each remaining corner.

*Quilting holds the 3 layers (top, batting, and backing) of the quilt together and can be done by hand or machine. Our project instructions tell you which method is used on each project. Because marking, layering, and quilting are interrelated and may be done in different orders depending on circumstances, please read the entire **Quilting** section, pages 138 - 141, before beginning the quilting process on your project.*

TYPES OF QUILTING
In the Ditch Quilting
Quilting very close to a seamline or appliqué is called "in the ditch" quilting. This type of quilting does not need to be marked. When quilting in the ditch, quilt on the side opposite the seam allowance.

Outline Quilting

Quilting approximately ¼" from a seam or appliqué is called "outline" quilting. Outline quilting may be marked, or you may place ¼"w masking tape along seamlines and quilt along the opposite edge of the tape. (Do not leave tape on quilt longer than necessary, since it may leave an adhesive residue.)

Ornamental Quilting

Quilting decorative lines or designs is called Ornamental Quilting. This type of quilting should be marked before you baste quilt layers together.

MARKING QUILTING LINES

Fabric marking pencils, various types of chalk markers, and fabric marking pens with inks that disappear with exposure to air or water are readily available and work well for different applications. Lead pencils work well on light-color fabrics, but marks may be difficult to remove. White pencils work well on dark-color fabrics, and silver pencils show up well on many colors. Since chalk rubs off easily, it's a good choice if you are marking as you quilt. Fabric marking pens make more durable and visible markings, but the marks should be carefully removed according to manufacturer's instructions. Press down only as hard as necessary to make a visible line.

When you choose to mark your quilt, whether before or after the layers are basted together, is also a factor in deciding which marking tool to use. If you mark with chalk or a chalk pencil, handling the quilt during basting may rub off the markings. Intricate or ornamental designs may not be practical to mark as you quilt; mark these designs before basting using a more durable marker.

To choose marking tools, take all these factors into consideration and **test** different markers on **scrap fabric** until you find the one that gives the desired result.

USING QUILTING STENCILS

A wide variety of precut quilting stencils, as well as entire books of quilting patterns, are available. Using a stencil makes it easier to mark intricate or repetitive designs on your quilt top.

1. To make a stencil from a pattern, center template plastic over pattern and use a permanent marker to trace pattern onto plastic.
2. Use a craft knife with a single or double blade to cut narrow slits along traced lines (**Fig. 21**).

Fig. 21

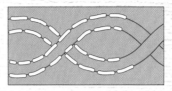

3. Use desired marking tool and stencil to mark quilting lines.

CHOOSING AND PREPARING THE BACKING

To allow for slight shifting of the quilt top during quilting, the backing should be approximately 4" larger on all sides than the quilt top. Yardage requirements listed for quilt backings are calculated for 45"w fabric. If you are making a bed-size quilt, using 90"w or 108"w fabric for the backing may eliminate piecing. To piece a backing using 45"w fabric, use the following instructions.

1. Measure length and width of quilt top; add 8" to each measurement.
2. If quilt top is 76"w or less, cut backing fabric into 2 lengths slightly longer than the determined **length** measurement. Trim selvages. Place lengths with right sides facing and sew long edges together, forming a tube (**Fig. 22**). Match seams and press along 1 fold (**Fig. 23**). Cut along pressed fold to form a single piece (**Fig. 24**).

Fig. 22	**Fig. 23**	**Fig. 24**

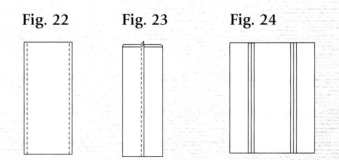

3. If quilt top is more than 76"w, cut backing fabric into 3 lengths slightly longer than the determined **width** measurement. Trim selvages. Sew long edges together to form a single piece.
4. Trim backing to correct size, if necessary, and press seam allowances open.

CHOOSING AND PREPARING THE BATTING

Choosing the right batting will make your quilting job easier. For fine hand quilting, choose a low-loft batting in any of the fiber types described here. Machine quilters will want to choose a low-loft batting that is all cotton or a cotton/polyester blend because the cotton helps "grip" the layers of the quilt. If the quilt is to be tied, a high-loft batting, sometimes called extra-loft or fat batting, is a good choice.

Batting is available in many different fibers. Bonded polyester batting is one of the most popular batting types. It is treated with a protective coating to stabilize the fibers and to reduce "bearding," a process in which batting fibers work their way out through the quilt fabrics. Other batting options include cotton/polyester batting, which combines the best of both polyester and cotton battings; all-cotton batting, which must be quilted more closely than polyester batting; and wool and silk battings, which are generally more expensive and usually only dry-cleanable.

Whichever batting you choose, read the manufacturer's instructions closely for any special notes on care or preparation. When you're ready to use your chosen batting in a project, cut batting the same size as the prepared backing.

ASSEMBLING THE QUILT

1. Examine wrong side of quilt top closely; trim any seam allowances and clip any threads that may show through the front of the quilt. Press quilt top.
2. If quilt top is to be marked before layering, mark quilting lines (see **Marking Quilting Lines**, page 139).
3. Place backing wrong side up on a flat surface. Use masking tape to tape edges of backing to surface. Place batting on top of backing fabric. Smooth batting gently, being careful not to stretch or tear. Center quilt top right side up on batting.

4. If hand quilting, begin in the center and work toward the outer edges to hand baste all layers together. Use long stitches and place basting lines approximately 4" apart (**Fig. 25**). Smooth fullness or wrinkles toward outer edges.

Fig. 25

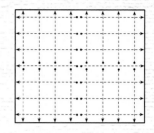

5. If machine quilting, use 1" rustproof safety pins to "pin-baste" all layers together, spacing pins approximately 4" apart. Begin at the center and work toward the outer edges to secure all layers. If possible, place pins away from areas that will be quilted, although pins may be removed as needed when quilting.

HAND QUILTING

The quilting stitch is a basic running stitch that forms a broken line on the quilt top and backing. Stitches on the quilt top and backing should be straight and equal in length.

1. Secure center of quilt in hoop or frame. Check quilt top and backing to make sure they are smooth. To help prevent puckers, always begin quilting in the center of the quilt and work toward the outside edges.
2. Thread needle with an 18"-20" length of quilting thread; knot 1 end. Using a thimble, insert needle into quilt top and batting approximately $^1/_2$" from where you wish to begin quilting. Bring needle up at the point where you wish to begin (**Fig. 26**); when knot catches on quilt top, give thread a quick, short pull to "pop" knot through fabric into batting (**Fig. 27**).

Fig. 26   Fig. 27

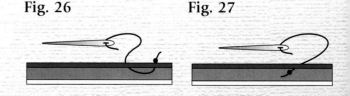

3. Holding the needle with your sewing hand and placing your other hand underneath the quilt, use thimble to push the tip of the needle down through all layers. As soon as needle touches your finger underneath, use that finger to push the tip of the needle only back up through the layers to top of quilt. (The amount of the needle showing above the fabric determines the length of the quilting stitch.) Referring to **Fig. 28**, rock the needle up and down, taking 3 - 6 stitches before bringing the needle and thread completely through the layers. Check the back of the quilt to make sure stitches are going through all layers. When quilting through a seam allowance or quilting a curve or corner, you may need to make 1 stitch at a time.

Fig. 28

4. When you reach the end of your thread, knot thread close to the fabric and "pop" knot into batting; clip thread close to fabric.

5. Stop and move your hoop as often as necessary. You do not have to tie a knot every time you move your hoop; you may leave the thread dangling and pick it up again when you return to that part of the quilt.

MACHINE QUILTING

The following instructions are for straight-line quilting, which requires a walking foot or even-feed foot. The term "straight-line" is somewhat deceptive, since curves (especially gentle ones) as well as straight lines can be stitched with this technique.

1. Wind your sewing machine bobbin with general-purpose thread that matches the quilt backing. Do not use quilting thread. Thread the needle of your machine with transparent monofilament or coordinating general-purpose thread if you want your quilting to blend with your quilt top fabrics. Use decorative thread, such as a metallic or contrasting-color general-purpose thread, when you want the quilting lines to stand out more. Set the stitch length for 6 - 10 stitches per inch and attach the walking foot to sewing machine.

2. After pin-basting, decide which section of the quilt will have the longest continuous quilting line, oftentimes the area from center top to center bottom. Leaving the area exposed where you will place your first line of quilting, roll up each edge of the quilt to help reduce the bulk, keeping fabrics smooth. Smaller projects may not need to be rolled.

3. Start stitching at beginning of longest quilting line, using very short stitches for the first ¼" to "lock" beginning of quilting line. Stitch across project, using one hand on each side of the walking foot to slightly spread the fabric and to guide the fabric through the machine. Lock stitches at end of quilting line.

4. Continue machine quilting, stitching longer quilting lines first to stabilize the quilt before moving on to other areas.

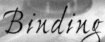

Binding encloses the raw edges of your quilt. Because of its stretchiness, bias binding works well for binding projects with curves or rounded corners and tends to lie smooth and flat in any given circumstance. It is also more durable than other types of binding.

MAKING CONTINUOUS BIAS STRIP BINDING
Bias strips for binding can simply be cut and pieced to the desired length. However, when a long length of binding is needed, the "continuous" method is quick and accurate.

1. Cut a square from binding fabric the size indicated in the project instructions. Cut square in half diagonally to make 2 triangles.

2. With right sides together and using a $^1/_4$" seam allowance, sew triangles together (**Fig. 29**); press seam allowance open.

Fig. 29

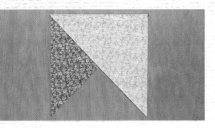

3. On wrong side of fabric, draw lines the width of the binding as specified in the project instructions, usually $2^1/_2$" (**Fig. 30**). Cut off any remaining fabric less than this width.

Fig. 30

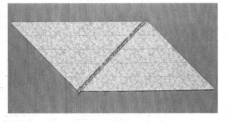

4. With right sides inside, bring short edges together to form a tube; match raw edges so that first drawn line of top section meets second drawn line of bottom section (**Fig. 31**).

Fig. 31

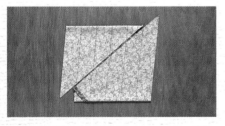

5. Carefully pin edges together by inserting pins through drawn lines at the point where drawn lines intersect, making sure the pins go through intersections on both sides. Using a $^1/_4$" seam allowance, sew edges together. Press seam allowance open.

6. To cut continuous strip, begin cutting along first drawn line (**Fig. 32**). Continue cutting along drawn line around tube.

Fig. 32

7. Trim ends of bias strip square.
8. Matching wrong sides and raw edges, press bias strip in half lengthwise to complete binding.

ATTACHING BINDING WITH MITERED CORNERS

1. Press 1 end of binding diagonally (**Fig. 33**).

Fig. 33

2. Beginning with pressed end several inches from a corner, lay binding around quilt to make sure that seams in binding will not end up at a corner. Adjust placement if necessary. Matching raw edges of binding to raw edge of quilt top, pin binding to right side of quilt along 1 edge.
3. When you reach the first corner, mark $^1/_4$" from corner of quilt top (**Fig. 34**).

Fig. 34

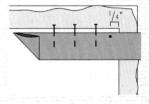

4. Using a $^1/_4$" seam allowance, sew binding to quilt, backstitching at beginning of stitching and when you reach the mark (**Fig. 35**). Lift needle out of fabric and clip thread.

Fig. 35

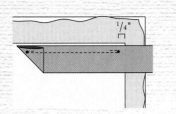

Fig. 39 **Fig. 40**

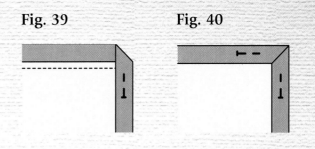

5. Fold binding as shown in **Figs. 36** and **37** and pin binding to adjacent side, matching raw edges. When you reach the next corner, mark $1/4$" from edge of quilt top.

Fig. 36 **Fig. 37**

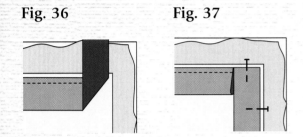

6. Backstitching at edge of quilt top, sew pinned binding to quilt (**Fig. 38**); backstitch when you reach the next mark. Lift needle out of fabric and clip thread.

Fig. 38

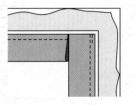

7. Repeat Steps 5 and 6 to continue sewing binding to quilt until binding overlaps beginning end by approximately 2". Trim excess binding.
8. If using $2^1/2$"w binding (finished size $1/2$"), trim backing and batting a scant $1/4$" larger than quilt top so that batting and backing will fill the binding when it is folded over to the quilt backing. If using narrower binding, trim backing and batting even with edges of quilt top.
9. On 1 edge of quilt, fold binding over to quilt backing and pin pressed edge in place, covering stitching line (**Fig. 39**). On adjacent side, fold binding over, forming a mitered corner (**Fig. 40**). Repeat to pin remainder of binding in place.

10. Blindstitch binding to backing, taking care not to stitch through to front of quilt (**Fig. 41**). To make Blind Stitch, come up at 1. Go down at 2 and come up at 3. Length of stitches may be varied as desired.

Fig. 41

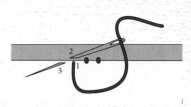

MAKING A HANGING SLEEVE
Attaching a hanging sleeve to the back of your wall hanging or quilt before the binding is added allows you to display your completed project on a wall.

For Quilts With Binding
1. Measure the width of the wall hanging top and subtract 1". Cut a piece of fabric 7"w by the determined measurement.
2. Press short edges of fabric piece $1/4$" to wrong side; press edges $1/4$" to wrong side again and machine stitch in place.
3. Matching wrong sides, fold piece in half lengthwise to form a tube.
4. Follow project instructions to sew binding to quilt top and to trim backing and batting. Before blindstitching binding to backing, match raw edges and stitch hanging sleeve to center top edge on back of wall hanging.
5. Finish binding wall hanging, treating the hanging sleeve as part of the backing.
6. Blindstitch bottom of hanging sleeve to backing, taking care not to stitch through to front of quilt.
7. Insert dowel or slat into hanging sleeve.

For Quilts Without Binding

1. Follow **For Quilts With Binding**, Steps 1 and 2, page 143.
2. Matching right sides, fold piece in half lengthwise to form a tube. Using a $^1/_2$" seam allowance, sew tube; turn and press.
3. Blindstitch top and bottom edges of hanging sleeve to backing, taking care not to stitch through to front of quilt.
4. Insert dowel or slat into hanging sleeve.

Embroidery Stitches

Blanket Stitch

Come up at 1. Go down at 2 and come up at 3, keeping thread below point of needle (**Fig. 42**). Continue working as shown in **Fig. 43**.

Fig. 42   **Fig. 43**

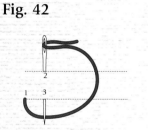   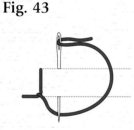

French Knot

Follow **Figs. 44 - 47** to complete French Knots. Come up at 1. Wrap thread twice around needle and insert needle at 2, holding end of thread with non-stitching fingers. Tighten knot; then pull needle through, holding floss until it must be released. For larger knot, use more strands; wrap only once.

Fig. 44   **Fig. 45**

Fig. 46   **Fig. 47**

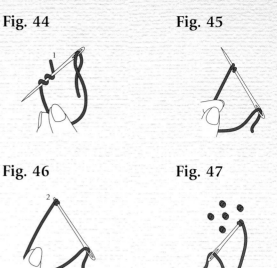

Running Stitch

The running stitch consists of a series of straight stitches with the stitch length equal to the space between stitches (**Fig. 48**).

Fig. 48

Metric Conversion Chart	
Inches x 2.54 = centimeters (cm)	Yards x .9144 = meters (m)
Inches x 25.4 = millimeters (mm)	Yards x 91.44 = centimeters (cm)
Inches x .0254 = meters (m)	Centimeters x .3937 = inches (")
	Meters x 1.0936 = yards (yd)

Standard Equivalents					
$^1/_8$"	3.2 mm	0.32 cm	$^1/_8$ yard	11.43 cm	0.11 m
$^1/_4$"	6.35 mm	0.635 cm	$^1/_4$ yard	22.86 cm	0.23 m
$^3/_8$"	9.5 mm	0.95 cm	$^3/_8$ yard	34.29 cm	0.34 m
$^1/_2$"	12.7 mm	1.27 cm	$^1/_2$ yard	45.72 cm	0.46 m
$^5/_8$"	15.9 mm	1.59 cm	$^5/_8$ yard	57.15 cm	0.57 m
$^3/_4$"	19.1 mm	1.91 cm	$^3/_4$ yard	68.58 cm	0.69 m
$^7/_8$"	22.2 mm	2.22 cm	$^7/_8$ yard	80 cm	0.8 m
1"	25.4 mm	2.54 cm	1 yard	91.44 cm	0.91 m